Who Pays for Diversity?

Who Pays for Diversity?

WHY PROGRAMS FAIL AT RACIAL EQUITY AND WHAT TO DO ABOUT IT

Oneya Fennell Okuwobi

UNIVERSITY OF CALIFORNIA PRESS

University of California Press
Oakland, California

© 2025 by Oneya Fennell Okuwobi

Library of Congress Cataloging-in-Publication Data

Names: Okuwobi, Oneya Fennell, author.
Title: Who pays for diversity? : why programs fail at racial equity and
   what to do about it / Oneya Fennell Okuwobi.
Description: Oakland : University of California Press, [2024] |
   Includes bibliographical references and index.
Identifiers: LCCN 2024044584 (print) | LCCN 2024044585 (ebook) |
   ISBN 9780520392212 (cloth) | ISBN 9780520392229 (paperback) |
   ISBN 9780520392243 (ebook)
Subjects: LCSH: Diversity in the workplace—United States. | Racial
   justice—United States. | Minorities—Employment—United States. |
   Race discrimination—United States—Prevention.
Classification: LCC HF5549.5.M5 O425 2024 (print) | LCC HF5549.5.M5
   (ebook) | DDC 331.13/30973—dc23/eng/20241126
LC record available at https://lccn.loc.gov/2024044584
LC ebook record available at https://lccn.loc.gov/2024044585

ISBN 978-0-520-39221-2 (cloth)
ISBN 978-0-520-39222-9 (pbk.)
ISBN 978-0-520-39224-3 (ebook)

34 33 32 31 30 29 28 27 26 25
10 9 8 7 6 5 4 3 2 1

For every employee who has ever been called a diversity hire.

To my nonacademic readers: Feel free to skim chapter 1. You're here for the stories and solutions starting in chapter 2. I won't tell if you don't.

Contents

Acknowledgments

This book has been a labor of love. That is only possible because so many loved me through the process of writing it. Whether you are mentioned by name, if you ever offered me a smile, encouraging word, or gentle push, know that this is for you too.

In everything I do, God gets first thanks. It is because of Your grace that I care about making this world more like the very good one You created. I hope that this book does at least a little of that.

Deepest thanks to my mentor, advisor, and friend Korie Little Edwards. With you, I've never had a moment when my scholarship felt unseen or unsupported. I appreciate your careful comments to shape this work. It is a privilege to glean from your brilliance. Our fancy dinners, deep conversations, and spiritual kinship are a joy. Here's to many more years of this great work we get to do.

Thank you to Elaine Howard Ecklund. You are a mentor par excellence. I and many scholars stand on your broad shoulders, and we all smile when you say you are proud of us. You help make people possible, and I am grateful.

To Vincent Roscigno, Steven Lopez, David Melamed, Eric Schoon, Hollie Nyseth Nzitatira, and so many more at The Ohio State University, thanks for always being there to propel my scholarship forward, ask hard questions, and be a listening ear. Vinnie, you are such a fantastic sounding board; I think you may be thanked in half the work in our discipline, and I am grateful to have had your input here. Thanks also to the G-15 cohort. You exemplified what it means to encourage one another in a collegial environment. I continue to learn from each one of you through the work you produce and the people you are.

To my colleagues at the University of Cincinnati: Erynn Masi de Casanova, Jeffrey Timberlake, Anna Linders, Steve Carlton-Ford, Danielle Bessett, Katherine Castiello Jones, and Littisha Bates, thank you for creating and recreating a department that I am so proud to be a part of. It is a privilege to know you. Special thanks to my friend and colleague Letisha Engracia Cardoso Brown. You've been a book buddy, adventure partner, and co-conspirator in all the best ways.

I am grateful for the Religion and Public Life Program, its fellows past and present, and everyone I had the opportunity to encounter at Rice University. Special thanks to Rachel Schneider and Jacqui Frost; you were the best people to be postdocs with!

Thank you to Michael O. Emerson for introducing me to sociology and encouraging me to take a chance on academia.

Thank you to Naomi Schneider, Aline Dolinh, and all the wonderful folks at University of California Press who supported this book in coming to fruition.

I am very thankful to James M. Thomas and Sarah Mayorga for your comments on the book manuscript and your continued coaching through the revisions. Your insight made all the difference.

Thanks to the undergraduate research assistants who spent hours deidentifying transcripts and scheduling interviews. I couldn't have done it without you!

Tribe Collective! We are indeed on the move. A group of Estranged Pioneers making a difference. I hope this work represents you well. Grateful for your friendship and wisdom.

Thank you to Christopher N. Beard for reintroducing me to the idea of racial justice within the church and for being a pastor and friend. Thanks also to every pastor and leader I've had the chance to work with toward churches like heaven.

Thanks to the Louisville Institute, the Society for the Scientific Study of Religion, the Black Faculty Association at the University of Cincinnati, and the Charles Phelps Taft Research Center for supporting this work.

Thank you to the directors, mentors, and fellow cohort members of the inaugural Stanford University CASBS Summer Institute on Diversity Science for helping me open the aperture.

Thank you to my parents, Regan and Elaine Fennell, for your love and support. You taught me to know and love who I am. You also stretched to ensure I took advantage of every opportunity to learn something new, from musical instruments to trips abroad to gourmet foods. You shaped my intellectual curiosity; this book is only possible because of you. To my brother Omari, I'm so proud of the man you are and so grateful that we can inspire each other to good works. To Grandma Ruth Fennell, Grandpa Roosevelt Rhodes, Grandma Mary Rhodes, Uncle (Junie) Roosevelt E. Rhodes, Jocie Fennell, and my niece and nephew Kiersten and Kendrick, there aren't enough pages here to talk about the supportive words, the laughs we've shared, or the love that holds our family together, so I'll simply say thank you.

To my husband OlaDele Okuwobi, a heartfelt thank you for being a true partner. I remember when we were sitting on the beach in Mexico deciding whether I should take the leap into sociology. I'm glad we said yes! Happy to know there's at least one person who cares about my facts. Love you bunches.

Thank you to my daughter, Cadence. You are a powerful woman and the world would be a better place with more leaders like you. My scholar heart rejoices that you read this book cover to cover, annotated it, and gave me great feedback. My mama heart rejoices that you have taken the lessons contained herein to heart and have learned to resist some of the highest costs of diversity. There is no limit to what you can do and I'm just glad to be here for it.

Finally, thank you so very much to every pastor, professor, and professional who was kind enough to share your story with me. We laughed and we commiserated in those interviews. Through the gift of your accounts, I was able to craft this work. You are each so worthy of respect and dignity. May you always and only be in workplaces that provide it.

1 The Costs of Diversity

I just found out that the university president named me by name in an open letter in response to George Floyd's murder as an example of what the university is doing to end racism on campus. My contract hasn't even started, and they've already tried to turn me into a token.

ASSISTANT PROFESSOR OF ISLAMIC STUDIES

Odessa Flint was a hotly desired commodity for her university. A precise scholar with perfectly coiffed locks and a steady presence, Flint would be a great addition to any school because of her accomplishments in scholarship and teaching. But her work was not the only reason her university wanted to hire her. The university was facing accusations of racism, which seemed to be validated by the lack of Black faculty members. Because of this, they were overjoyed that she accepted an assistant professorship with them. She recalls, "They're excited, you know, they have all these issues going on, and they know how white their department is, right? And they know it's not a good look, to have a predominantly white, overwhelmingly white faculty."

Without her permission, or even knowledge, Flint's image became a symbol for diversity. One afternoon, she received a text from a friend of hers who was a professor at another university. Flint's picture was on the screen in a diversity, equity, and inclusion presentation to tout all the great programs her university had for faculty of color. "They're going out to other universities and making presentations about all the great things they're doing about faculty of color to promote retention. Got your picture on a slide. You know, look, we got all these Black scholars this year and we're doing so great, and we are a model."

Being on a slide in a presentation probably would have been fine, except that Flint had not received the promised benefits of the programs the university was promoting. "It's taken six months for them to do the things that they promised they would do. And in the meantime, I feel like many of us are kind of falling in between the cracks." The difference between promise and reality made Flint question the university's commitment to her and other scholars of color. "But when you really get into the inner workings, it's kind of like they're not following up."

In addition to being displayed as a symbol of diversity, Flint herself had to take on significant committee work to display that diversity. She puzzled, "Different committees that they have me on, I'm like, why the hell am I on this committee? My first or second year, I was on a hiring and recruitment committee. Some people may feel like that's really an honorable position to be in. I felt like it was wasting my time." It is highly unusual for an assistant professor to be on a university-wide committee in their first year. Flint felt the reason she was chosen was clear. The university would benefit from claiming a Black committee member. "But the sense that I got was that the deans are looking at the faculty who are on these hiring committees, and asking why they are all white. You got to pull somebody in."

The work Flint performed on these committees took away from her time to conduct research. This matters in academic careers, because research, most often measured by the number of publications authored, is the key metric on which many professors are evaluated. Assistant professors who fail to be productive enough in their research will fail to achieve tenure, or a permanent academic position. Some assistant professors who do not get tenure are able to move to other universities, while many are not only out of a job but also have to switch careers. Flint worried, "My time for research is always overwhelmed. That's just how it is."

Although Flint knows her research is the metric that matters most to the university, and counts most toward her prospects of tenure, she gives away even more time that could be spent on research because she has chosen to prioritize her commitment to students. This is because the metric that matters most to *her* is supporting the graduate students who need it. Driven by philanthropic self-sacrifice, Flint gives her time and energy to graduate students who would not receive mentorship elsewhere. "I have so many graduate students who have come to me this year. It's very much like, we need somebody to come in and save us, because the people here, they don't understand us. If we want to talk about race, they don't understand what we're doing intellectually. So, from grad students, that was pretty clear."

Another difficulty that Flint faces is feeling like she cannot be herself within the academy. While she sees the way that her image is valued in presentations, she does not feel that value extends to the rest of her presence. Flint explained, "I don't feel like I can be myself anywhere in the academy. I think it's always a struggle. It's just, you feel like you're incompatible with what they believe a professor should be or what they should look like or how they should act." Not being able to be herself led Flint to the conclusion that she needs to have two identities. One that is herself and one that is for the sake of the university. "I think you always feel like you're multiple people, kinda schizophrenic. Because if I could really be myself, I would be able to say things without feeling like there's going to be retribution."

The weight of these issues strained Flint's mental and physical health, but she didn't expect there to be any change in the future. "And I think it's because it's more faculty of color focused, nobody really cares."

Flint's experience, and that of others in this book, illustrates who pays for diversity. For the most part, it is the employees of color who are used as the face of it. Flint was hired, in part, to deflect charges of racism at her university. Then, similar to the professor quoted in the epigraph to this chapter, she was used as a symbol of racial progress to boost the university's reputation as a leader in diversity and inclusion.[1] Flint was further pulled onto committees to display demographic representation, even when this work was inappropriate to her career stage. At the same time, Flint lacked the support she needed for her scholarship, her students, and her advancement. As a result, Flint was required to do more labor on committees relative to her colleagues; she was concerned about the hypocrisy of her workplace; and she was prevented from living out an integrated racial and scholarly identity. Meanwhile, the university gained an excellent scholar and the ability to boost its reputation.

Diversity, for universities and other workplaces, can be defined as representing, including, or involving people from different racial backgrounds in such a way as to connote racial equality. Organizations that appear to embrace racial diversity can benefit hugely: they experience a reputation boost and are able to attract new customers. For example, they may be insulated from charges of racism by pointing to the physical presence of people of color as somehow representative of harmonious race relations.[2] Criticisms of diversity, equity, and inclusion programs have become more popular in recent years; however, even when diversity is vilified, people of color are used to legitimate these attacks.[3] Workplaces receive benefits from just appearing to be diverse—whether or not their demographic realities align with the image they project. To this end, organizations both liberal and conservative benefit by making people of color highly visible, as in Flint's case. And yet, while diversity is often discussed in terms of benefits to people of color, employees may receive little or nothing compared to how much their workplaces benefit, and may in fact pay huge costs.

The costs of diversity are the heart of this book. Over the course of two years, I spoke to employees of color within churches, universities, and corporations that promote racial diversity. These employees described how actions done in the name of diversity affected their careers, families, and personal well-being. Diversity programs are commonly reported by workplaces to improve conditions for employees of color; this is not the full picture. Employees of color report that most diversity initiatives are done to benefit the workplace (in terms of money, status, customers, etc.), often without regard to actions that would actually bring about equitable conditions for employees. That some diversity, equity, and inclusion programs are being dismantled as they come under challenge only underscores that they were focused on organizational, not employee, benefits.[4] In this book I focus on the experiences of employees of color to show the negative, unexamined ripple effects ignored in crafting diversity initiatives. In doing so, I bring visibility to how diversity is being used, what action it is driving, and, importantly, how it is affecting racial equity.

Diversity and Me

My first experience with the negative, unintended consequences of diversity initiatives occurred at the tender age of seventeen. I attended a high school so wonderfully nerdy that our Battle of the Brains (BOB) squad always dominated the competition.[5] One of my classmates and I gained admission to the Ivy-est of the Ivies and celebration broke out in our AP chemistry class. The celebration was cut short for me when another student said with a smile, "You only got in because you're Black." From the time I was a child, my parents told me, "You will have to work twice as hard to get half as far." That day, I realized that even when I arrived at the places my hard work, a little luck, and a middle-class family socialization afforded me, my efforts would be undermined still. Elite schools gain in reputation by having a diverse student body. What is a positive for the university, other observers reframe as a detriment on the bodies of color representing that diversity. Because of the way diversity has been portrayed, I was subject to unwanted scrutiny and deemed undeserving regardless of my qualifications.

By no means was this my last encounter with diversity imperatives. As a finance manager at a Fortune 50 company, I was asked to be on a diversity committee within six months of joining the company. I continued to do diversity work on behalf of women and people of color for the balance of my career. I was thrilled to help and could not understand why my white coworkers considered it a chore. "Don't put so much time into this," I was advised by a white male whom I entered the company with. When I asked why, he was adamant: "They don't care about this stuff—it will not help you advance." I heard the advice, but I could not heed it; the work seemed too important to let drop. Others cycled on and off these various committees, but I remained a constant fixture. I conducted trainings and recruiting drives while seeing relatively little movement in metrics of diversity climate or racial representation during my fourteen years with the company.

During my time in corporate finance, I completed a Master of Divinity degree. Eyeing a career change into full-time ministry, I was disappointed to find there were limited opportunities for me as a woman. I quickly found that the easiest way into the pulpit was as a speaker on diversity. There, my racial qualifications outweighed my gender disqualifications. For ten years, I read social science books as a hobby (I told you I was a nerd), combining sociology and theology to show churches the importance of becoming a "multi-ethnic" church that included people from all racial groups. While I continue to believe in this core message, I have been chastened by the negative effects that churches trying to become multiethnic had on pastors of color.

A few years ago, people of color working for racially diverse churches began to pull me aside after my presentations at conferences, asking if I'd join them for lunch or coffee. As I spent time with them, they told me about their experiences one by one. Some felt as though they were not being heard. Others felt they were only brought in to show a Black or Brown face and were not permitted to be themselves. Still others were experiencing symptoms of ill health because of their jobs. To a person, each brought up their church's diversity initiatives as a contributing factor to their difficulties. The first time it happened, I was startled. The next time, I was angry. The third time, I knew there was work to be done. This book, examining the effects of diversity imperatives on employees of color, became a necessity after it literally walked up to me in the form of employees in pain.

These negative experiences with diversity take me back to conversations around my family's dining room table. My maternal grandfather, who was the first Black milkman in his Virginia town, has spent every Thanksgiving I can remember lamenting the loss of segregated institutions. His fond memories of Black doctors, dentists, churches, and schools made me wonder whether something has been lost. Indeed, this is a challenging time for racial affinity organizations, with Historically Black Colleges and Universities (HBCUs) experiencing declining enrollment and Black churches losing their younger members.[6] If we sacrifice these institutions on the altar of diversity, are we progressing or regressing?

People of color are best positioned to answer this question. Without their perspective, diversity programs might be hailed as a clear success. After all, they succeed at bringing value to firms through the business case for diversity, which is the commitment to racial, gender, and other forms of representation based on benefits to the bottom line. They succeed at bringing additional congregants to churches and students to universities. They succeed at driving creativity when people from various backgrounds bring their perspectives to bear on innovation challenges. But these successes fall woefully short if they do not bring about equity. By equity, I mean everyone has what they need to flourish because there is "fairness in processes, practices, and outcomes within the context of historical, economic, social, and institutional forces that have resulted in an unequal playing field."[7] Ultimately, diversity programs fail because persistent racial inequity remains in almost every measurable area.

What's more, by making representation the primary goal, and believing that racial equity will follow, diversity draws away important energy that could otherwise be directed toward the needs of employees of color. At their worst, diversity initiatives develop into another way that the possessions of people of color, in this case, their very racial identity, become the province of white people and organizations. The employees I spoke with saw diversity initiatives, even at their best, as "smoke and mirrors," both showy and ineffective.

Affirmative Action to Diversity

Despite escalating challenges to diversity programs, diversity as a concept remains incredibly popular with the public.[8] Diversity was born as the kinder, gentler alternative to affirmative action. After the Civil Rights victories of the 1950s and '60s, affirmative action programs appeared at universities and workplaces to remedy previous discrimination. This push to positively and aggressively remove barriers of discrimination met with controversy; such programs were, and still are, legally and politically challenged.

One such challenge, *Regents of the University of California v. Bakke*, was litigated in the US Supreme Court in 1978.[9] The plaintiff was denied admission to medical school and contended that affirmative action in the form of racial quotas was unfair. Justice Lewis Powell wrote the controlling opinion in this case, which allowed universities to maintain race-conscious admissions for the purpose of enabling learning through diversity, even if the university had not previously been complicit in racial exclusion. He established that the "goal of achieving a diverse student body is sufficiently compelling to justify consideration of race in admissions decisions." This ruling created a government interest in having students from all walks of life engage with one another—an interest in promoting diversity. To comply with the court's ruling, universities altered their language from affirmative action, under which universities could be explicit about past discrimination, to that of diversity. While affirmative action actively worked to repair past harms, the language of diversity touts the benefits of togetherness for all without respect to inequality. This diversity imperative gained widespread acceptance and became a cornerstone for many institutions of higher learning.[10]

Workplaces arrived at a similar destination regarding diversity via a different path. There, affirmative action arose from Lyndon Johnson's 1965 Executive Order 11246 to take "affirmative action" to ensure no discrimination with regard to "race, color, religion, sex, or national origin." This order had little effect until the 1970s, when it was supported by legal enforcement and a host of newly hired equal-opportunity experts within companies.[11] The term of affirmative action was short-lived, however. Beginning in the 1980s, the Reagan administration began to loosen equal opportunity enforcement. This left the human resources departments committed to equal opportunity efforts scrambling to remain organizationally relevant. To maintain the necessity of these departments, they shifted focus toward "diversity management," a term coined in the early 1980s. Diversity management recast the representation of women and people as a competitive advantage for companies. The metrics that offices now used to denote successful diversity initiatives, unlike those used under affirmative action, were self-generated and self-regulated with little ability to address racial inequality in recruiting, retention, and promotion.[12]

Churches have been slower to diversify when compared with universities and workplaces. Since 2000, however, cultural and demographic factors, such as increases in the percentage of racial minorities and cues from other institutions, have enabled the number of multiracial religious organizations to quickly multiply. The number of multiracial churches in the United States (defined as those in which no racial group comprises more than 80 percent of the congregation) made up fewer than 7 percent of churches in 2000; by 2019, this number had more than doubled, with the largest percentage change among white evangelical congregations.[13] Racially diverse congregations encompass a broad spectrum of differences in neighborhood composition, leadership identity, religious tradition, and worship style. What they have in common is that they meet the accepted form of diversity, which is bringing people of color into majority white spaces. None of the growth in multiethnic congregations has come from white congregants switching to majority-minority spaces.[14]

As of 2023, however, the unstable foundation on which much diversity work was based has been compromised. In twin cases challenging admissions policies at the University of North Carolina and Harvard University, the US Supreme Court ruled these schools' use of race in admissions unconstitutional, largely undoing the *Bakke* precedent and the legal cover for organizations to create diverse environments. It is expected that court cases challenging the consideration of race in other venues, such as workplaces, will rapidly follow. We are at a crossroads regarding how organizations will or may consider race in the future. In this period of flux, advocates of purposeful action to achieve racial equity may admit that diversity initiatives have a mixed record. While an interest in diversity has allowed some continued focus on race, progress in areas such as work discrimination, occupational status, wealth, and education gaps has stalled.[15] Since *Bakke*, diversity initiatives have been divorced from the rationale of racial inequality. Perhaps as a result, diversity initiatives themselves have had a role in "sustaining and legitimating inequality."[16]

Diversity Ideology

To understand the effects of diversity initiatives in churches, universities, and workplaces, it is critical to understand the ideology underlying them. Ideology here means "systems of meaning, concepts, categories and representations which make sense of the world."[17] Sociologist Sarah Mayorga-Gallo studied neighborhoods to articulate four tenets of diversity ideology pervasive among white people and institutions.[18] The first, *diversity as acceptance,* promotes the celebration of different cultures, particularly via food and music. *Diversity as intent* allows virtue to be achieved through the intention to develop racially inclusive relationships, whether or not such relationships ever develop. *Diversity as liability* focuses on the problems and tensions of diversity. It includes exerting control over "diverse" spaces so that they remain comfortable for whites. *Diversity as commodity* treats people of color as resources for white people and organizations. This last tenet is a core focus of this book as it produces many, though not all, of the costs of diversity. Examining commodification spotlights how practices driven by diversity ideology affect work for employees of color.

Commodification here is defined as "the treatment of Asian, Black, Latinx, and Native peoples as objects rather than humans for the benefit and satisfaction of others, namely white people."[19] Recall from the story of Odessa Flint at least three ways in which she was commodified. First was her hiring after accusations of racism on campus, second was the use of her picture without permission in a diversity presentation, and third was her assignment to committees to represent demographic diversity. All these actions satisfied the need of the university and its leadership to appear a diverse, inclusive, and not racist space. These specific actions were not about Flint, the person, and all that she brings in her expertise. Instead, these actions were about the object "Black woman faculty member" that provides something the organization needs.

Commodification is not hidden away as some shameful secret; it is inherent to the business case for diversity, which is a popular justification for increasing demographic representation of certain groups. The business case for diversity is "the proposition that a diverse workforce is essential to serve a diverse customer base, to gain legitimacy in the eyes of a diverse public, and to generate workable solutions within a global economy."[20] Per this definition, the business case is that employees of color will serve customers of color and help their workplace's reputation—here, diversity is an economic, not a moral, imperative.[21] Managers and shareholders should therefore embrace representation of women and people of color because their presence will provide a competitive advantage. Notably, benefits to workers are absent from this definition.

And the business case for diversity has proven true. Management scholars Quinetta Roberson and Hyeon Jeong Park demonstrate that diversity improves companies' performance in capital markets. This means that companies with a reputation for diversity receive legitimacy and additional capital to fund their businesses. These measures are largely based on external reputation. Roberson and Park found no impacts on production outcomes that would have more to do with interactions within the firm. So, regardless of the interactions within a diverse company, firms receive some benefits just by seeming to be diverse.[22]

In churches, too, commodified diversity can drive positive results for the organization. Sociologists Jessica Barron and Rhys Williams's ethnography of Downtown Church revealed how the church used Black volunteers to make it clear that they were not a boring, all-white church.[23] Black congregants, especially attractive Black men, were placed right by the door to make the church seem an exciting and authentic downtown organization. Still, Black people lacked power within the organization and were precluded from positions of influence. The diversity of Downtown Church was ultimately shown to perpetuate hierarchies that demean Black people.

Finally, colleges and universities commodify diversity by striking "the diversity bargain" with white students. Sociologist Natasha Warikoo finds that white students value diversity because students of color have something to teach them. Supporting diversity then becomes about consuming an educational environment improved by the presence of people of color.[24] Universities, in turn, benefit by being able to paint themselves as diverse places. These symbolic representations of diversity make universities seem progressive, global, and elite.[25]

Reexamining Diversity

The gains that commodification provides to white people and institutions, at the expense of people of color, prompt serious reexamination of diversity as it exists. Some scholars have already begun this process. With their push for "critical diversity" in workplaces, sociologists Cedric Herring and Loren Henderson list several strategies including the following: "advocate an expansive notion of diversity, but seek out distributive justice that will serve to assist 'disprivileged' groups; shift resources away from privileged groups, especially when invoking the rhetoric of diversity; and reconnect diversity to affirmative action and the need to offset historical and ongoing racial and gender discrimination, segregation, and bias."[26] Such efforts, they suggest, would explicitly address the racial inequalities that diversity ideology currently overlooks.

As Herring and Henderson suggest, any productive reimagining of diversity must seriously attend to the experiences of people of color. The perspective of employees of color as commodities within the project of diversity has been underinvestigated. As a number of scholars have begun to look at what diversity does, their primary focus has been at the organizational level. These investigations do not extend these effects of diversity policy to the people who are the object of them. Other work in this area has focused on the experiences of people of color in organizations but not always tied it back to diversity ideology. This includes investigations of token status, racialized jobs, racial discrimination, managing stigma, and investigation of Black people navigating white space.[27] Without attending to the actions that diversity ideology is driving, these studies miss a critical "why?" behind organizational outcomes.

Flatlining: Race, Work, and Healthcare in the New Economy by sociologist Adia Harvey Wingfield is one of the notable few books that focuses squarely on the experiences of people of color in diverse organizations. She examines the additional work, *racial outsourcing*, that accrues to Black doctors, nurses, and medical technicians because of the populations that hospitals seeking diversity fail to support. Here I build on her focused and nuanced account in medicine with a broad view across organization types and racial groups who are objectified by diversity. As Wingfield finds, most high-status Black employees "do not necessarily encounter daily, overt expressions of racial bias. However, these professionals may be attuned to the ways structural and cultural processes work to their disadvantage."[28] Commodification is the one among those processes that I here examine in depth. In addition, Wingfield's compelling focus is on what happens when organizations want a diverse client base and expend limited or no institutional resources to support it. I home in on the other side of the coin, namely what happens to employees of color when organizations instead spend their resources on external displays of diversity designed to garner organizational benefits.

Perhaps part of the reason that relatively few works connect the experiences of people of color in organizations, particularly negative experiences, to diversity ideology is that diversity initiatives are viewed as the solution, not part of the problem. Certainly I am not advocating that we go back to the days of enforced segregation. But, what if the prescription of diversity ideology—integration—will inevitably keep us from effectively treating the disease of racial inequity? What if we downplay the negative effects of diversity just because of the promise that it could work? Going forward, we have to become comfortable with the possibility that diversity initiatives are a net negative to the work of racial justice instead of somewhere between neutral and positive.

There is already evidence that the work of racial justice is hindered by an ideology of diversity. Diversity as a term is ambiguous, and as such, those using it may have a difficult time addressing real problems of race in organizations. Organizations may use the term diversity as a way to avoid other terms, particularly racial equity. Moreover, diversity ideology and its focus on the celebration of difference obscures the underlying inequalities that exist before people come into the organization. By blinding organizational members to racial inequality, ideas of diversity can make nonsensical solutions to it.[29] That is why people can simultaneously support diversity and oppose solutions to the inequalities that led to lack of representation in the first place.[30]

Critical scholarship has approached diversity in different ways, but almost never abandons it altogether. One approach has been to see diversity as necessary but not sufficient. As sociologist Ellen Berrey writes in her groundbreaking book *The Enigma of Diversity,* "The drive for diversity serves as a partial but insufficient answer to the unfinished project of racial justice."[31] Another approach is to differentiate between surface-level and more comprehensive forms of diversity in, for example, legal scholar Nancy Leong's comparison between thin and thick diversity.[32] She defines thin diversity as only having to do with representation, whereas thick diversity would include the relationships between people. These approaches suggest that we need to go further, rather than positing that we may be on the wrong road.

Another approach, so common that it is often mentioned in passing, is the idea that diversity initiatives do little to nothing for racial equity. One examination of diversity work and the British police force concluded that their efforts were "window dressing . . . the policies are not seen as helpful, nor even harmless, but as pernicious in that they contrive to give the appearance of progress, while actually achieving little."[33] As sociologist Victor Ray, in his influential *Harvard Business Review* article, states: "Diversity policies ostensibly aimed at equalizing opportunity have done little to alter the overall distribution of organizational power and resources."[34]

I argue instead that diversity initiatives actually shift the "distribution of organizational power and resources" even further in the direction of those who already have them. This occurs through commodification, which uses the presence and the work of employees of color to visibly display diversity for the benefit of their workplaces. In a racialized society where the majority of organizations are controlled by white people, the commodification of people of color for organizational enrichment will inevitably reinforce the current racial hierarchy. As a result, even the most progressive and inclusive diversity practices feature racial inequality.

I further suggest that the efforts spent on painting organizations as diverse do not leave the inside untouched, but instead actively diminish internal effectiveness. After all, if diversity work is mere "window dressing," what of those whose job it is to dress the windows? Like Odessa Flint, employees of color enlisted in organizational diversity work see both the outside perspective and the inside reality and are affected by the differences between the two. Moreover, employees of color are often compelled to offer their work and even their likenesses to display diversity for parties outside the organization, the audiences for the window dressing.

The contradictory images that employees of color encounter reduce internal legitimacy. "Legitimacy" refers to rightness and acceptability, and has often been applied to whether organizations are doing what is generally accepted by their field. "Internal legitimacy," however, refers to the rightness of organizations' actions as judged by stakeholders within them.[35] It is lost as companies do not conform to employees' expectations of them.[36] This matters to employers and employees alike; loss of internal legitimacy harms organizational identification and attachment, and even the psychological health of employees.[37]

Whether the negatives of diversity practices outweigh the negatives of the version of the multiverse in which diversity practices are not in place, is a question beyond the scope of this investigation. We will be unable to even engage that question, however, if we fail to acknowledge how diversity ideology and the practices informed by it cost employees of color. Pursuit of the better starts with clear recognition of the current state.

Listening to Employees of Color

When it comes to who pays for diversity, my husband and I have lamented, while we do laundry together, that "every Black pastor in a multiracial church has a story." It is common knowledge among our network of friends and family who have seen and supported so many pastors through burnout and back to health. Through careful fieldwork, I have concluded that Asian engineers and Latino/a professors too pay for diversity in their bodies, minds, and emotions. Their stories of commodification and harm, broken promises, and even longing for belonging live just beneath the surface. My hope is that this book will prompt more people, including their employers, to ask to hear these stories and to act accordingly.

Starting in the fall of 2019, I set out to obtain a broad view of organizational diversity practices through their effects on employees of color. I interviewed employees across three organization types: churches, universities, and corporations. For comparability, the employees I spoke to in each organization type were the equivalent of entry-level managers. I also reviewed information from the websites of the organizations these employees work for and interviewed independent diversity professionals for this analysis. In all, I talked to sixty employees and another three key informants spanning fifty-three organizations (see appendix for participant demographics and interview guide).

By relying on three organization types, I make clear that the effects of diversity ideology on employees of color are not isolated to certain niches. There is not a greener pasture in one industry or another because each of these realms is affected by diversity ideology. To the extent that commodification under diversity ideology disadvantages employees of color in for-profit and nonprofit, large and small organizations alike, it is a mechanism of racial inequality affecting most employees of color. Commodification thereby holds nonnegligible power in reinscribing the current racial order. Because of this, I encourage readers representing one organizational type or another that there is something to learn here, whether the venue described is a college, corporation, or church. The experiences of employees of color across these workplaces are more alike than not alike.

Throughout this book, I refer to diverse organizations. I do not use this term uncritically, but recognize the meanings diversity has taken on, both positive and negative. Recall that for purposes of this study, diversity can be defined as representing, including, or involving people from different racial backgrounds in such a way as to connote racial equality. By extension, diverse organizations are those undertaking these representations. While all the organizations in this study do have some degree of demographic diversity, my referring to them as diverse does not rely on a given level of representation. Likewise, when I refer to diversity, I am not referring to demographic diversity unless so specified, but rather the meanings and functions that fall under the term diversity. I have used the promotion of diversity as the standard for diverse organizations because I believe it is the marketing of diversity, the need of an organization to portray itself as diverse, that is producing the effects I see in this study.

The ways that diversity is incorporated into organizational identity vary. Workplaces may incorporate diversity into their identity via vision and mission statements, statements to employees, website declarations, or other PR tactics. If I spoke to an employee who indicated their employer had no interest in diversity (which I asked within the first ten minutes of the interview), I discontinued the interview. Given the prevalence of diversity ideology within corporations and universities and the recruiting standard used for churches, this only occurred in two instances.

I connected with employees in a variety of ways. Beginning with personal contacts in each of the organizational types, I used snowball sampling, allowing interviewees to connect me with other respondents to build trust ahead of interviewing.[38] This trust was critical given the tenuous position of early-career employees of color. To ensure I heard from voices in each of the major census regions, I also recruited from organizational websites, particularly those of churches. Finally, I used social media platforms including Twitter and LinkedIn to connect with people who might be willing to share their stories. All named participants in this book are given pseudonyms; other participants are identified by their organization type, region, and racial identity.

One group of interviews was with associate pastors in Protestant churches. The term associate pastor here encompasses any non-head clergy, including those working in children's, youth, music, women's, or adult ministry. With demographic changes, the idea of diversity within churches has taken on tremendous value, prompting numerous books, consultants, conferences, and other resources. The embrace of diversity has also brought a new group of employees of color into majority white churches; one of the key pieces of advice for churches looking to become multiracial is to empower diverse leaders.[39] Churches whose employees took part in this study are churches that have indicated via their mission, vision, or values a specific goal of being a diverse organization. Churches do not always use the word "diverse," and may in fact be vehemently against it, so examples of this might be a vision or mission statement including the terms "multiethnic," "multiracial," "racially reconciling," "all people," or "all nations."

Universities and workplaces concentrated on serving middle-class whites are more uniformly focused on diversity than churches, so there was no mission or vision requirement for those organizations during recruiting. I did probe during interviews for indicators of an outward commitment to diversity. Professors were tenure-track assistant professors at predominantly white institutions. All universities were nonprofit, selective institutions, and could be public or private. These institutions have had a near universal consensus about the importance of diversity, although it is beginning to erode.[40] Corporate employees worked for companies in a variety of sectors, including health care, finance, and transportation. I interviewed management-level employees as diversity policies and practices tend to ignore hourly employees.[41] Entry-level managers would be analogous to the level of an associate pastor or assistant professor.

My sample comprises US-based individuals who identify as Black, Asian, or Latino / a and have worked in their organization for at least one year. Throughout most of this work, I have chosen to focus on similarities across the experiences of employees of color. Many scholars and activists, rightfully so, take issue with the racial flattening accomplished by the phrase "people of color." When it is employed to avoid saying "Black" or to deny the distinct experiences of racialization each group has, this lumping together is indeed harmful. In the present case, I believe it has been more helpful than harmful, by showing the remarkable costs that result up and down the racial hierarchy from employing diversity within organizations.

Via the ethnoracial variation in my sample, I can compare the experiences of different groups. An open question remains as to whether diversity policies particularly reproduce anti-Blackness; there is evidence that being commodified by diversity affects Black people more than other nonwhite groups.[42] Examining multiple groups allows me to compare the level to which commodification and any resultant costs are part of each group's experience. I turn to that question in chapter 4.

The employees I spoke with would be deemed middle class or above. It is therefore important to note the ways this investigation is a classed as well as a racialized one. Sociologist William Julius Wilson details how affirmative action policies created opportunities for middle-class Blacks while leaving lower socioeconomic status Blacks truly disadvantaged.[43] This is one place where diversity is similar to affirmative action. Today, diversity policies mostly target management ranks, making any costs that crop up primarily costs of the middle class.

Studying inequality within the middle class, as in this investigation of diversity, is just as pressing as studying the increasing segregation that relegates Blacks and Latino / as to lower-performing schools and less wealthy neighborhoods. As sociologist Barbara Reskin conceptualized, there exists a complex system of über discrimination with a web of disadvantage.[44] Because of this, racism remains intractable when we deal with only one issue at a time. If we only disentangle the sticky strand of racism that seems most urgent at a given moment, we will quickly be trapped by another.

Given the ubiquity and uses of diversity, it is an important part of shaping the racial structure and worthy of immediate attention.

My goal in each interview was to hear from employees how they understand their organization's efforts toward diversity, how the organization's understandings of diversity align with their own, and what their experiences were in a diverse organization. The interviews, scheduled for sixty to ninety minutes, were structured to collect similar information from each respondent while allowing for variation. The interviews covered how employees came to join the organization, their alternatives, specific interactions with diversity policy and discourses within the organization, and their relationships with people at all levels within the organization. Participants were also asked whether they experience any advantages or disadvantages as a result of their employers' diversity initiatives. Finally, the employees were asked to examine how diversity and race relate in their experience.

One focus of these interviews was to detail any costs that employees of color might experience related to diversity practices. By costs, I simply mean disadvantages that accrue to people of color as a result of their commodified presence within a diverse organization. This language of costs is intentionally broad; there are a number of places that these costs can appear. People of color experience monetary costs when slotted into diversity roles supporting the image of an organization as diverse.[45] Even in roles not specifically related to diversity, people of color may be tasked with the labor of making their organization seem diverse at the expense of their productivity.[46] Students at "diverse," predominantly white institutions experience costs to their identity, developing a lower sense of self and belonging than those at HBCUs.[47] People of color also experience relational costs when they are embedded in demographically diverse networks but do not receive the same access to resources as others in the same network.[48] In addition, people of color may experience costs to success in leadership roles when their power to enact their own strategic imperatives is limited, or when they are placed in leadership over a failing organization.[49]

This book centers experiences of commodification, and other costs driven by diversity ideology, rather than racial discrimination more generally. Recall, commodification is when people of color are treated as objects and not people so that others benefit in some way.[50] Accounts of commodification include being inserted into meetings, pictures, or work teams to display diversity; being hired expressly to deflect charges of racism or signal a commitment to diversity; and doing the work to teach whites about diversity, race, and racial identity. The effects of commodification also extend to how others react to employees of color because they have been made symbols of diversity. For example, the backlash foisted on a "diversity hire" who is assumed incompetent because they were brought in under a diversity imperative.

Employees of color do not just recount what they experience in these interviews, but also how they make sense of those experiences. Diversity ideology, as it has been currently defined, focuses on white people and organizations. This has left an open question as to whether people of color simply understand that this ideology exists and respond to it, or whether they hold their own ideology. I was able to probe this question by ascertaining how well the organizational strategies of employees of color aligned with diversity ideology.

I also discussed with employees of color why they opt into these organizations to begin with. In most cases, the answer was more complicated than "I needed a job." After all, employees, particularly those in religious organizations and to a lesser extent those in university settings, have alternatives to these diverse organizations. When I delve into why employees of color come and stay, I probe how the disprivileging of organizations associated with people of color continues to create a drive to diversity. From institutions such as the Black church and HBCUs, to organizational departments such as Latino / a Studies, the lower levels of resources afforded to these entities push people of color to join majority white organizations. When other opportunities are foreclosed, employees of color are more likely to see diversity as an opportunity, even as their choices are being limited.

Goals for This Book

In chapters 2 and 3, I argue that employees of color face disadvantages as a result of their commodified presence within diverse organizations. Chapter 2 examines tokenism and commodification to compare how diversity ideology and colorblind racism operate in the lives of employees of color. This comparison reveals how neoliberalism, which places faith in the free market to set the value of human interactions, upholds both colorblind racism and diversity ideology. Neoliberalism is often thought of in economic terms, but it is also a profoundly racial project that explains why innovations in racial ideology produce minimal results in terms of racial progress.[51] In chapter 2, I also advance the idea of *diversity displays*, which are the appearance of activities around diversity, even if such activities are divorced from appropriate outcomes for people within the organization.

Chapter 3 shows the consequences of paying for diversity. In it, I return to the effects of commodification outlined in chapter 2 to detail how the heavy work demands, threatened legitimacy, and subjugated identity characteristic of commodification harm the physical and emotional well-being of employees of color. In chapter 4, I then compare the experiences of commodification across racial groups, showing how diverse organizations value the racial capital of Black, Latino/a, and Asian employees differently.

In chapter 5, I turn to diversity ideology, finding a distinct diversity ideology for people of color as opposed to white people and institutions. I name the three tenets of this ideology: *diversity as philanthropy*, *diversity as opportunity*, and *diversity as resource*. Through diversity as philanthropy, employees of color explain why they remain in diverse spaces despite the costs to themselves. They use religious rationales, their own experiences, and altruism as reasons to stay in their organizations in hopes of creating a better space for those who will come after them. The outcomes of diversity as philanthropy show the penalty that workers rejecting neoliberal economic maximization will pay in their careers. The two other tenets, diversity as opportunity and diversity as resource, are two sides of the same coin. Diversity as opportunity is what happens as employees of color allow their racial capital, or value derived from racial identity, to accrue to their workplaces in exchange for a position for themselves. Diversity as resource, however, is enabled when employees of color find themselves in a structural position of strength and determine to profit off their own racial identity.

Finally, I focus on the organizational implications of these findings. Chapter 6 draws from theory on racialized organizations to show how the attractiveness of diverse organizations is enhanced by status differences between organizations. Often people of color opt into organizations marketed as diverse because they are viewed as higher status than majority-minority organizations, those in which people of color predominate and lead, such as HBCUs. Employees of color hope to benefit from that status bump but are not always able to in the long term. In chapter 7, I detail formal organizational diversity initiatives and their effectiveness for employees of color. Pervasive programs such as diversity training, mentorship, and diversity offices fail to consider data that could maximize their efforts, leaving a gap in support for employees of color.

I conclude *Who Pays for Diversity?* by returning to my central argument: that diversity ideology and the logics it informs undermine racial justice to reproduce white supremacy. By being honest about the costs of diversity, instead of trying to do diversity better, we can move toward better alternatives. I end on a hopeful note by offering policy recommendations that can shift organizations away from commodification and toward equity.

2 Commodities and Tokens

In an episode of the short-lived sitcom *Mixed-ish*, two Black women in a law office spin a wheel to determine which of the limited roles each gets to play.[1] One winds up with the role of "office show pony." The announcer excitedly explains: "Your boss will trot you around the world to prove he's not a racist! He'll introduce you to Black clients whose cases you aren't even handling, and you get to become the face of the company on bus benches downtown."[2] Based on the accounts of the employees I spoke with, this description is much closer to reality than fiction.

Ayodele Marshall, a wealth manager in the southern United States, knows exactly what it is like to be the office show pony. When I spoke with Marshall via Zoom, he was surrounded by palm trees in an outdoor space that resembled a resort. I later found out that this was his home. Marshall considers his house a point of pride and uses it extensively in entertaining. During his six years in finance, Marshall has often hosted catered events for his staff and their families. The tangible spoils of his job belie a more complex lived reality in daily work.

From the beginning, Marshall knew he would face challenges. His recruiters were up front that there was no charted pathway to success for a Black man in wealth management. "It was like, 'Hey, we've got to figure this out.' No one has an answer or solution." While he knew there would be difficulties related to race, perhaps in terms of bias or blatant racism, one thing he did not expect was the way his racial identity would be used by his employer. This commodification took the form of Marshall accepting awkward invitations to business meetings, only to discover that the client he has been asked to meet is also Black. "So, to fill out the diversity, they [my managers] want me to tag along. And I don't know why until we actually get there."

As a financial professional, Marshall wants to be prepared for any meeting that he is invited to. But because his management will not or cannot come out and say he is there to show the client that they have Black employees, Marshall is left to draw his own conclusions. He explained, "I had to figure it out as I was going through the proposals, meetings, the reviews, and everything with that. So, I kind of got it. I read in between the lines." In the process of trying to determine why he is needed for these client meetings and then preparing to be present in front of a client that is not his own, Marshall loses valuable time to complete his own work responsibilities.

Perhaps the most frustrating aspect of this commodification is that Marshall's coworkers do not admit it is happening, even when the circumstances of the meeting make it obvious. It becomes an infuriating open secret—everyone knows what is going on, but no one will say it out loud. "Sometimes it comes out and I say, 'I'm not really sure why I'm here.' They give me those politically correct answers: 'We need you as an extra set of eyes just to look over everything and make sure everything is correct.' And when I looked at it, I was like, 'We're all supposed to know this. You should know this as much as I do.'" Even his direct question is not met with a direct answer.

Being the face of diversity in ways that their white counterparts are not has four detrimental effects on Marshall and other workers who experience the same treatment: increased job demands, threats to personal legitimacy, threats to organizational legitimacy, and subjugated identity. In this chapter, I will first explain each of these four effects of commodification in turn. Then, referring to the chapter title "Commodities and Tokens," I will show how being commodified as the face of diversity is different than simply being a numerical token—someone in a demographic group comprising less than 15 percent of the organization. Finally, I will examine how commodification operates differently for women of color.

Commodification and Its Effects

The first effect of commodification that Marshall endures is increased job demands. High job demands can take the form of increased work, high psychological demands, and mismatches between effort and outcome.[3] Marshall takes time out of his workday to attend meetings with clients that are not his, leaving less capacity for the accounts he has been assigned, and adding pressure to accomplish his necessary tasks in a reduced amount of time. The extra time he expends on others' clients has little long-term benefit for Marshall because he does not always become part of their ongoing relationship management. For most, once he has shown his face, the job is done.

Marshall's experience of high job demands was shared by many employees of color I spoke with. Some call this the "minority tax" or "Black tax."[4] Derived from the concept of the cultural tax coined by psychologist Amado Padilla, the minority or Black tax refers to the extra, uncompensated work employees of color undertake on issues of diversity.[5] Or, as one professor put it, "spending all this time doing stuff that we don't really get recognized for." This might include serving on diversity taskforces, participating in meetings for no reason other than representation, or showing up for students and customers of color. These additional burdens result in a higher level of occupational stress relative to white counterparts.[6]

The second thing that happens to Marshall is a threat to personal legitimacy. It is embedded in his comment, "I'm not really sure why I'm here." His experience of being brought along to meetings gives him a reason to question if it is his skills that make him valuable to the company or only his racial identity. Also known as differential legitimacy, the struggle for personal legitimacy is another cost that employees of color endure.[7] An organization's focus on diversity often stigmatizes minoritized folks as others assume they were hired to fill a race-based slot. When organizations tout their commitment to diversity as a badge of honor, it brands each employee of color with a question mark as to whether they deserve to be there. This threatened legitimacy lowers the status of employees of color in relation to their coworkers and can have the force of negating the claims of employees of color to organizational resources such as promotions and raises.[8]

Comedian Trevor Noah once joked about this in response to a diversity initiative by United Airlines. Recognizing that their field was 94 percent white and male, the airline announced plans to start a school that would be at least half women and people of color. Noah argued that this would be a great idea, if only it had not been publicized. "They shouldn't have announced this in the first place," he reasoned. "If you want to do something good, just do it; but no, they want a pat on the back for shit they should have been doing all along . . . because now you're undermining every new pilot you're going to have."[9] Noah went on to explain that passengers might be frightened to have Black and female pilots, assuming that they were "diversity hires" and therefore inherently unqualified.

This type of legitimacy threat to employees of color was expressed well by one Midwestern Latino assistant professor, who groaned, "You know, people say, 'Oh, you're just taking someone else's space. You're only here because you're the minority hire. You're only here because of affirmative action. You're only here because you're Puerto Rican.' Yeah, that's still prevalent." The response to this legitimacy threat forms the minority tax; employees of color work twice as hard to prove that they are not a diversity hire. The professor who was questioned about being hired for his race did exactly that, trying to be perfect to prove he belonged. "Well, it adds another level of scrutiny," he reasoned. "So, now I need to make sure all my i's are dotted, and all my t's are crossed, and that everything is right. There's an added pressure for me to prove myself to people." While the threat of being called a "diversity hire" may spur excellent performance, it also spurs additional stress and time wasted on tasks incidental to job performance to avoid accusations of incompetence. Because appeals to diversity lack the context of alleviating past discrimination, it is easy to frame diversity programs as an unfair advantage instead of seeing them rightly as a way to spotlight previously ignored job candidates of color.

When employees of color are commodified for their racial identity, this action also creates a threat to the internal organizational legitimacy of their workplaces. Internal legitimacy reflects how people within an organization feel about the rightness of their employers' actions. At the same time that Marshall asks why he is in a given meeting, he turns his questioning lens back onto the organization for putting him in that position. He asks his coworkers why he is at the meeting, and the need to even ask creates a threat to the internal legitimacy of the company that he works for. Actions that Marshall's company take to appear legitimate and diverse to those on the outside leave Marshall doubting the company's ethics. This questioning is accentuated by the fact that his coworkers won't 'fess up to what is being done, instead giving him a "politically correct" answer. It would be one thing if Marshall were brought in on the strategy, but since telling him "You're coming to this meeting because you're Black" could open management up to legal concerns, or at least awkward conversations, Marshall is expected to just play along.

Marshall's managers are concerned with demonstrating external legitimacy to clients and bring Marshall along to portray that they are a diverse firm. In the process, they damage their internal legitimacy since Marshall doubts the authenticity of his company's commitment to him as an employee. This conflict exhibits how external and internal legitimacy are interconnected.[10] Companies are often forced to choose between the two. In this case, diversity efforts designed to please external stakeholders jeopardize internal stability because they do not reflect the true state of the company. If the company were in fact demographically diverse, someone already on the client team could have been evidence of that, preserving both internal and external legitimacy. Instead, one of the few Black employees is pressed into a false show of racial representation. Beyond being deceptive, loss of internal legitimacy negatively affects companies via lower employee well-being and organizational attachment.

Finally, Marshall experiences subjugated identity. He admits that he would like to say more about his frustrations, but his desire to speak up has to be balanced with the need to maintain positive relationships at work. He reasoned, "There's a lot that I want to speak up on. But I also understand that there's a certain level of guardrails that I have, because I don't have any backup anywhere; it's just me." In an environment where everyone is willing to go along with the way he is treated, Marshall risks being thought of a troublemaker if he speaks up. He has decided that the better strategy is to remain silent so as not to slow his trajectory in the company. "If I'm going to speak out, I have to do it in the right context, because I don't want to end up limiting myself or limiting opportunities ahead, just because I say the wrong thing to the wrong person or I say something that may be against the context or against the status quo, or make everyone else uncomfortable, even though I may be right." Knowing that he is right is not enough. As a cost of being an employee of color within a diverse company, Marshall feels cornered into making sure others are not uncomfortable by forgoing his own comfort.

Marshall biting his tongue is one example of the racial tasks employees of color must undertake to maintain smooth interactions in a diverse workplace.[11] When employees of color do this, they experience subjugated identity: they are not allowed to align with their preferred identity in the workplace and are instead constrained to what the organization needs them to be. Constantly monitoring what they can and cannot say is part of this role. One tiny mistake can have detrimental consequences. A Black manager at a transportation company was reminded of this the hard way. He is a younger manager, hired just out of college, and he has already been taught not to use his preferred language on the job.

So, I slipped up. We got let out at 4:30 on a Friday and I didn't hear the announcement. So, I saw my coworker getting up and she says, "I am out of here." I was like, "We're getting out at 4:30? Okay, bet." Then one of my other coworkers mocks me and she's like, "oh okay, bet" and she calls me "a ghetto little hoodrat."

One little word, "bet," and the subsequent mocking were enough to remind this employee that he needs to be on his guard. Any indication of being outside the established workplace culture could be a career-harming mistake. When I asked him how he felt in the face of his coworker's rudeness, he responded, "Upset, secluded, excluded, and suppressed."

People of color already experience challenges to identity because of racism that gives rise to *double consciousness*. Coined by the sociologist and educator W. E. B. Du Bois in 1897, double consciousness is a response to the conflict between the negative, race-based appraisals of others and the positive appraisals of oneself and one's own community.[12] With respect to the experiences of Black people, this means seeing yourself and others who share your racial identity as having intelligence and worth, but also knowing that others may project their own image onto you.[13] Du Bois calls double consciousness a gift because it subverts the racist social structure, denying its false claims of Black inferiority. He acknowledges it is also a curse. The disconnect between your view of yourself and that of others divides identity into coexisting and alternative versions of oneself. You know that the way other people see you is not true, but you cannot ignore it; the views of others affect your thoughts and the way you present yourself.[14]

Subjugated identity adds an additional challenge. It is similar to double consciousness in that it is an undesirable intrusion on identity formation by others. It is distinct, however, in that its end is commodification. To be commodified, the identities of employee of color are shaped into what the organization needs. The key considerations are what will gain the organization legitimacy, what will sell, and especially, what version of nonwhiteness will not offend white sensibilities. This subjugation of identity damages the coherence of carefully managed racial identity with negative consequences for self-esteem and belonging.[15] Employees experiencing subjugated identity may change their manner of speech, conversation topics, style of dress, and even their hair to enact an acceptable form of their racial identity. This benefits the organization by providing the right image of nonwhiteness to show off. At the same time, it leaves employees walking on eggshells to be seen as the person others want to see.

High job demands, threatened legitimacy, and subjugated identity are the experiences of commodification for employees of color. These negative effects result from the habitual objectification of these employees' racial identity for the benefit of others. Things as seemingly innocuous as being brought along to a meeting for no reason other than race become detrimental when repeated time and again. When commodified, people become a resource rather than retaining their value as individuals.

This commodification creates powerful negative reactions from those subject to it. When employees of color talked to me about how it feels to be a commodity, I was surprised at how visceral their emotions were. I recall one interview with a Latino pastor working to bridge between Mexican and white congregants of his church, neither of which was his culture. When I asked how he felt about it, he simply shouted at the top of his lungs, "I HATE IT." Similarly, when I asked a Black pastor, who had been the diversity guy in both secular and religious organizations, what he would tell a young pastor considering a church that promoted diversity, he yelled, "RUN!" The emotions evoked by commodification are not surface level. They are real, deeply held, and evidence of the harm taking place beneath the polished portrayals of diverse workplaces.

While employees of color experience the harms introduced above, white people and institutions, conversely, receive benefits. The benefits of commodification to organizations can be financial, such as through the awarding of contracts made possible by bringing employees of color along to important meetings. They can also be reputational. For example, *Fortune* publishes an annual list of the "top 20 Fortune 500 companies on diversity and inclusion."[16] Companies rely on lists such as this one to tout their diversity credentials when compared to their peers. One particularly ironic example of this is Wells Fargo. Wells Fargo appeared on the most recent diversity list and tweeted their pride at this honor.[17] What they did not tweet about, however, is that they have been the subject of multiple racial discrimination lawsuits in hiring and lending.[18] Numerical representation of people of color allows Wells Fargo to promote a "proud tradition of diversity" on their website while obscuring court filings that tell a different story. Sociologist Matthew Hughey finds that white organizations use people of color in a similar way to improve their reputations.[19] His studies of both white *antiracist* organizations and white *supremacist* organizations show that their members spotlight Black friends to exempt themselves from charges of racism. In each of these cases, people of color are celebrated not as people but for what the presence of their nonwhiteness represents.

Diversity Displays

The value of diversity as a commodity drives *diversity displays* that help realize the value of diversity for the organization.[20] Diversity displays provide the appearance of inclusion of underrepresented groups, even if these displays themselves are divorced from positive outcomes for those groups. The sole purpose of a diversity display is the display itself, whether through multiracial photos, inclusion statements, or diversity trainings. In one of the most notorious examples of a diversity display, the University of Wisconsin photoshopped student Diallo Shabazz into an image of white students attending a football game. Undeterred by the negative publicity in this case, York College took to Photoshop for a billboard of theirs, adding an Asian American student and one woman (who appears to be Muslim based on her head covering) to a billboard advertisement.[21] Diversity displays seek external legitimacy in the eyes of stakeholders and are enabled by objectifying people of color—those whose presence validates diversity claims. In the college cases above, only people's images were used. In many cases, however, people of color are required to physically appear, taking on additional visibility and labor for diversity displays to be successful.

Because diversity is more valuable for external appearances than internal ones, diversity programs can be valuable without tangible improvements for people of color.[22] This leads to two foci of diversity displays. The first is the numerical presence of diversity. Organizations claim that their diversity programs are designed to make sure various perspectives are included. In practice, however, the success of diversity initiatives is nearly always measured using statistics that track proportional representation of people of color.[23] Diversity statistics are unable to tell the full story. They may, for instance, mask a revolving door of people of color who exit the organization nearly as fast as they enter. However, because simply demonstrating numerical diversity leads to the benefits thereof, such as improved market value and external legitimacy, organizations can afford to pay less attention to substantive diversity or the quality of interactions and opportunities within the organization for all.[24]

A second focus is the appearance of activity around diversity. Diversity initiatives are not equal because not all activity yields results for the targets of initiatives. By the early 1990s, diversity management became commonplace within corporate America, with 70 percent of Fortune 500 companies boasting diversity programs. However, the diversity program implemented most, diversity training, has been shown to be the least effective at improving results for women and people of color within companies.[25] In universities too, there is a pervasive mismatch between diversity policy judged to be good and whether that diversity program actually changes organizational culture over time.[26] This is not to say that organizations intentionally set out to implement ineffective programs. However, with limited resources to satisfy both external and internal stakeholders, the balance tilts toward stakeholders outside the organization.

Racialized labor forms the display case for diversity displays, concentrating the appearance of diversity by constraining employees of color to certain tasks and departments within workplaces. Racialized labor is labor that is purportedly neutral but disproportionately distributed by race. One way this occurs is by assigning employees of color to career pathways that primarily support other people of color. Sociologist Sharon Collins details this occurrence in her 1997 book, *Black Corporate Executives*.[27] She shows how Black professionals were shunted into jobs supporting specialized markets of Black clients and customers. These specialized paths curtailed opportunities for advancement to the top level of organizations. What's more, these jobs were more vulnerable, especially in economic downturns, leading to less economic stability for Black employees. With racialized labor, companies get the benefit of having a Black employee to work with their Black clients, bolstering claims of diversity. The employee bears the downside in their job security and prospects for advancement.

Over twenty years since the publication of *Black Corporate Executives*, Oladele Marshall finds himself in the exact same situation that Collins describes. Besides participating in diversity displays on client meetings, he also serves majority Black constituencies day in and day out. Marshall pays for this assignment because his clients tend to have smaller accounts. Smaller accounts are nearly inevitable given the wealth gap between whites and Blacks. Marshall said of the places he is assigned: "These locations have very low performance. And that's in any industry that I see. A lot of corporate America, whether that's for-profit, nonprofit, usually the minority workers are in the areas that are having the most challenges. They won't put someone like me in a high-growth scenario or high-performance area." Because he serves a majority-minority area, Marshall struggles to meet his professional goals. Meanwhile, this work provides his employer the opportunity to claim that they maintain a diverse clientele.

Tokens or Commodities: Comparing Diversity
Ideology with Colorblind Racism

Typically, when the experiences of employees of color are discussed, and often in situations of racialized labor, the word token comes up. There are many ways in which this word is appropriate. After all, diversity displays use employees of color as a token, or visible representation, of diversity. The stories of these employees nearly always involve them being the only member of their racial group, or one of a few, in their workplace.

Sociologically, the term token is used to refer to someone underrepresented in a demographically skewed organization. Management expert Rosabeth Moss Kanter's scholarship on tokens argues that when someone is in a demographic group that makes up less than 15 percent of the organization, they have particular experiences related to being in the minority. She names the effects of being tokens as hypervisibility, boundary heightening between tokens and the rest of the group, and having the tokens trapped in certain roles. Her work helped clarify that characteristics being associated with women in the workplace were not feminine qualities, but those of people who are subject to the performance pressures that tokens experience.

Since Kanter, other studies have challenged the idea that demographics alone lead to tokenism. The negative effects of tokenism are not always related to proportions within the organization. The status of tokenized individuals and the level of threat their presence offers to the majority group create negative consequences that do not disappear at the 15 percent threshold. For example, women in professions not considered typical of them, like police work, continue to experience hypervisibility and boundary heightening even as their ranks grow. Also, white men in the minority tend not to experience the effects of being a token when in female-dominated roles.[28]

Accounts of the employees I spoke with also challenge the idea that being a numerical minority is enough to create the conditions of being a token. As Kanter herself notes, tokens serve as "representatives of their category." For this to happen, something beyond being among the only ones in your category must be true. Why would an organization want to highlight the one Black person in a department if there were nothing to be gained from it? This is where the benefits of appearing diverse comes into play. For an organization to portray itself as diverse requires people of color to represent some valued identity for the purpose of financial gain. Because diversity is valuable, organizations are incented to hold up their employees of color as representatives of their group. It is perhaps this focus that creates hypervisibility, rather than being one of a few, which can be cause for invisibility.

While Kanter wrote in the period before diversity management, she includes in her account elements of commodification. For example, she describes one woman whose office show pony experience happened when her management made her sport a corsage and allow her vice president to escort her to a lunch celebrating women in business. As Kanter observed, this act "gave the company brownie points but cost nothing."[29] Conversely, it cost the woman her dignity and made her feel like she was sent on a date with her vice president. Kanter's analysis, however, focused on proportions rather than company imperatives as the source of difficulties for her tokens. What if the issues of the numerical minority are as attributable to their company's need to display them as to their minority status?

To distinguish the experience of being made a representative of one's group for financial gain from simply being in the minority, I use the term commodity. This term follows the tenets of diversity ideology. By signaling the ties to monetary gains, "commodity" begins to get at the mechanisms creating negative experiences for people of color in diverse organizations. The distinction between commodities and tokens is important because if the issue is skewed demography, the solution to work issues experienced by employees of color is to bring in additional employees of color. The need to solve for numbers is an underlying assumption in many diversity initiatives focusing on increasing representation rather than workplace climate. The logic is that if representation comes, equity will naturally follow. If instead commodification is the issue, employees may continue to be objectified for the benefit of their organization long after their racial group is proportionally represented in the organization. The solution then lies in changing the financial incentives for diversity.

Although commodification is what people experience when there is a focus on diversity, this does not mean that employees are necessarily better off where diversity motives aren't ascendant. When employees of color are in an organization not focused on diversity, their experiences may instead be marked by colorblind racism. Sociologist Eduardo Bonilla-Silva calls colorblind racism the most predominant racial ideology of the post–Civil Rights era.[30] It operates by minimizing race and denying that structural racism exists. Within this ideology, race should not matter, so people tend to deny or explain away its continuing effects. Colorblind racism differs from diversity ideology because while the former denies a problem exists, the latter leaves room for a problem but frames fair representation as the answer.[31]

It can be hard to disentangle issues of demography from other causes of marginalization because the drive for diversity often coincides with having employees who are demographically a small minority in their workplace. To gain insight on the difference between tokens and commodities, I spoke to a few employees who also had prior experience in organizations that did not focus on diversity. They were able to contrast their experiences between workplaces desiring a visible representation of diversity and workplaces where diversity was never mentioned. The comparisons of these employees illustrate how diversity practices differentially shape work experiences when the proportion of employees of color is relatively consistent.

The story of Jorge Morales highlights these differences. Morales moved from a church that espoused diversity to one that did not. Recall that most churches do not yet promote diversity, so it would not be unusual for a pastor to move between churches operating on different racial ideologies. Morales is a Puerto Rican in his late twenties whose loves include his family, Hot Cheetos, and Chicago sports. He is passionate about being a pastor and especially about helping teens and young adults. We met at his church on a day the offices were empty. Morales was wearing what he described as his typical dress—streetwear topped by a winter hat to protect his head from the chill in the room. He sported a pair of impeccably clean sneakers and a ready smile, as evidenced by the smile lines around his eyes. Morales spoke confidently, with the skill expected of a noted preacher, but would sometimes pause mid-story, surprised by the emotions betrayed by his voice. Our conversation lasted well beyond the scheduled hour as Morales described how he was treated in his jobs at different churches.

Morales first worked at a church that focused on diversity. This church is large and well known in the suburbs of a Midwestern city. The church desired to reflect diversity so they could reach out to a neighboring community that was increasingly Black and Latino/a. "They want to diversify. They wanted other opinions," said Morales. He moved from out of state to take a position there working with young adults. Although Morales was encouraged and excited about the new role based on what he was told during interviews, he soon discovered commodification underlying the diversity his church described during recruiting. He perceived a pervasive mismatch. "The church leadership didn't view diversity the way I did. It was more like, let's put this person here so we can appear diverse, so we can show representation. But when it comes to what we talk about, let's not."

The church's desire to reflect diversity played out in several ways. One area that Morales noted was who would be up front to lead worship, which in this case refers to the musical portion of Sunday services. He spoke about the machinations that occurred in replacing a worship pastor who resigned. The primary drive was to maintain the appropriate level of visual diversity.

"When I got there, the worship pastor had resigned. He was African American. And so, they were looking for an African American worship pastor." From the outset it was clear that the church was looking to replace a Black pastor with another Black pastor. Morales had some connections and offered to help. "Not knowing what they were looking for, I said, 'I have a friend, he's young, phenomenal worship pastor.' I sent them a video of him and it was said to me, 'Hey, which one is he in the video?' When I said, 'Oh, he's this one,' the response was, 'Oh, man. I was hoping he was this really dark one.'" Not only was a particular race or musical genre being requested but a particular shade. Being able to visually represent diversity meant that the person selected needed to appear dark enough to stand out to the audience on Sunday morning. The look mattered.

In the process of continuing to have the right look, the church went so far as to ship in Blackness rather than having the stage reflect the church's actual employee base. In the short term, the church decided to contract with out-of-state worship leaders rather than sacrifice their Sunday morning image. "We would rather plug in people so that we appeared [diverse]," Morales said. "In the last year, the church hired two African American worship leaders that lived out of state. They didn't even live here. But they were hired to come lead worship two times a month. And they were put on the staff page as worship leaders." Worship pastors typically do more than lead the Sunday morning experience. They also train new worship leaders and participate in church activities. Morales's church made it clear that community involvement could be sacrificed, but not image.

Commodification was not just something Morales saw in other positions; it was something he experienced personally. Although he is a gifted speaker who gives sermons across the country, his own church rarely called upon him to teach. This despite recruitment promises that he would be part of the regular teaching team who give sermons on Sunday mornings. Although he was not giving sermons, this didn't stop the church from putting Morales on stage.

Now, they loved me for announcements. I think it's because they loved how I looked. I think when they saw a Black face or Brown face, they were pumped to get it on stage. They strategically would say, all right, this person's doing announcements, and this person's on the worship team, so it'll look fully packaged. Easter, Christmas was hilarious. We would have one of the young worship leaders join the weekend team. And we would hire an African American. They would hire her to come out and lead worship so they would have a Black face on stage.

The careful curation of the stage on Sunday mornings formed its own sort of organizational blackface. Unwilling to do the work of making their staff look like the people they desired to reach, this church took shortcuts, focusing on the most important services of the year, to portray demographic diversity that was not even present.

Being commodified through showing his face for announcements, but not being able to do the preaching he was promised, threatened the church's internal legitimacy in Morales's eyes. Given the disconnect between words and actions, Morales was left with uncertainty about the rightness of his employer's behavior, which is one mark of the experience of commodification. This threat to internal legitimacy occurred because of the church's actions concerning the representation of people of color. Black worship leaders and even Morales himself were put in front of the congregation for show, but this did not represent reality behind the scenes.

Morales was also subject to the extra work and subjugated identity that come along with commodification. In terms of extra work, Morales was brought into projects outside of his area of responsibility. One project concerned the structure of the student ministry. The church was changing to have students meet in homes instead of centrally at the church. While Morales protested that the proposed model of ministry to students in homes would exclude students of color, the other pastors overruled him.

> And honestly, I'm just annoyed at being the token guy who's going to give you a perspective from a minority. It's annoying because it's like okay, I guess I'll be that guy. And I raised my hand and I say, "I think this is very organized. I think this is great. But I think it oppresses people of color. Guys, when I was in high school, if I was

a part of this model, my mom's not letting me go to that. You wanna know what she's gonna tell me? Whose house is that? We don't know them. And I said, honestly, my parents, we grew up where they had to protect us. And so, your white kids are going to be fine with it. They go to Suzy Q's house all the time. It's fine. They don't need to know what parents are there. Who's there? What uncle or what brother lives there? You are oppressing people of color with this." Yeah. It was just quiet.

Speaking up in this meeting was one of Morales's last stops on his way out the door. Ignoring the objections, the church decided to push through with meeting in homes. Morales's perspective was ultimately proven correct, as the strategy failed. Still, the negative response to his comments made him loath to speak up again in this way.

Facing constraints at his church, Morales continued to travel and preach as an outlet, an outlet it was agreed during his hiring he would continue to pursue. In an affront to his identity as a minister, his supervisors attempted to take this away from him. They complained that he looked tired and asked him to stop traveling. The weight of the combined experiences of commodification led to a level of anxiety that was unsustainable for Morales: "I had two anxiety attacks in my bathroom, and I thought I was dying. I went to the hospital. For the next thirty-six days, I didn't have an anxiety attack, but I had anxiety every night when I went to bed. I would go to bed like, 'okay, here we go.' I would fall asleep, wake up, cradle my head in my hands, cry and read Psalm 91." Never having had issues with anxiety, Morales was unsure with how to deal with this level of constant distress. "I wanted to die. I wasn't suicidal, but the thought of it, it felt like I wanted to die."

Morales got counseling and got healthy. The church even did a documentary about his "anxiety journey." Incidentally, Morales is one of *two* pastors in my sample who experienced anxiety attacks and then exhibited his healing for the same church that in large part caused the anxiety.

In all, Morales spent two years at this first church. The place he landed next was a more rural community church possessing "a culture that loves all people." This church was not focused on diversity. The lack of concern for diversity resulted in very different work experiences for Morales. One of the first things he noticed was that his race did not play a role in his hiring. He reasoned of his job offer, "And I believe they didn't hire me because I'm a minority. Yeah, cuz, it's not a part of their intentions yet . . . Do they like it? I don't know. I don't think they care."

However, the lack of concern over race introduced a different set of obstacles for Morales to navigate. In one conversation, Morales spoke up about the idea that the church was not reaching out to the communities of color nearby. The lead pastor took umbrage at Morales's comments and sought to show how he loved people regardless of their skin color. Instead of hearing Morales out, the lead pastor told Morales stories about two congregants of color that he had helped—one an undocumented immigrant, and another who was taken in by the lead pastor's family. The lead pastor was trying to illustrate his compassion across racial lines. For Morales, the pastor was illustrating something else: the pastor's disconnection from issues of race except when it came to those needing help. Morales attempted to show the lead pastor how narrow his approach was, saying, "I hear you, but every minority doesn't need you to come and rescue them. Some of them are executives in their jobs and they're not in this, like, situation where they need you to come save the day."

Morales's critique ultimately went unheard, as did his requests for the pastoral staff to engage in more education about race. He repeatedly asked that they watch a documentary about race to no avail: "I try to tell people, *13th* is the easiest thing to do. It's short. I mean, go read *The New Jim Crow*, my gosh, your mind will be blown. But like *13th* is visually great, creatively interesting, and just looks cool. It's easy for me to do, so once in a while I'll say 'Y'all need to watch *13th*.'" At the time of our interview, though, Morales wasn't anticipating reviewing the documentary with his colleagues; he was anticipating sending an email to ask why they had not watched it. "When my one-year hits in April, I'll have a real conversation. [I'll tell them] you've done none of the things."

Whereas Morales's experiences in the diverse church were marked by the commodification inherent in diversity ideology, his experiences in his second church reflected colorblind racism. Commodification under diversity ideology showed up when Morales was prominently placed on stage and had parts of his identity stripped when he was used for announcements rather than the preaching he was told he was hired for. Conversely, colorblind racism showed itself in the second church's indifference to Morales's racial identity. It was also evident in the lead pastor's lack of interest in issues of race; his refusal to interpret his lack of engagement as reflecting racial animus; and the oversimplification of racial philosophy to the prescription to treat everyone equally.

The bottom line is that neither diversity ideology nor colorblind racism benefits employees of color. However, to better understand the mechanisms of racial inequality, we must know how they operate differently. For Morales, colorblind racism provided partial relief to the commodification he experienced at his previous church. The upside was that he was no longer valued for his racial identity:

> I think over there [at my former church] they're like, "Your value on this staff is being a minority. You make us look good." I mean, I did good work. They liked what I did. But I had job security because I was a minority. I think here, I don't have the job security. I don't want that to be my job security. I don't want that. And I can be more me because they don't know what it's like to be around somebody [Latino]. I'm me. So, I feel like I have freedom here. I feel like I have a seat at a table to lead at a level, and that's not threatened because of my color.

Despite Morales's frustration with his current church's disengagement from issues of race, he preferred it to commodification. Not having to fill a role based on his race gave him more freedom if less job security. Morales was let go from the new church within a year after we spoke.

Not every employee saw this the same way. Others were glad for the opportunities and attention that diversity ideology lent them, despite their commodification. Aaron Chu is an Asian American pastor in a diverse church. Chu was asked to spend more than half of his working hours planning and executing services for the congregation, although as a counseling pastor he thought he would spend most of his time in sessions with congregants. While being part of the services took away from his primary responsibilities, he was asked to be there for Asian representation on the stage during Sunday morning service. Despite this clear commodification, Chu prefers it to the alternative. He finds that he is more likely to be ignored in settings where he is not being commodified. He reasoned, "Large context, because I'm the minority, I actually don't expect to be talked to. And the hard part is the ignoring hurts more than the blatant hate because that means they didn't even try." Chu would rather be acknowledged, even if the acknowledgment is negative.

Marginalization under the ideology of colorblindness is different from what results when someone is used as a resource for their organization's benefit. While the former is more in line with invisibility where the realities of race are ignored, the latter results in hypervisibility as race is publicly displayed. The harms of commodification and the sting of colorblindness can both occur in the presence of numerical tokenism. Morales's church experiences both happened on pastoral staffs with fewer than 15 percent people of color. In both cases he was demographically a token in a racially skewed organization, but only in one was he a commodity. Only in the church focused on diversity did he experience the hypervisibility, role limitation, and boundary heightening that have been associated with tokens. While demographic skews matter, the logics that drive organizational practice matter more. It is a logic of diversity, undergirded by diversity ideology, that leads employees of color to be representatives of their group.

On the surface level, a shift from colorblind racism to diversity ideology should be positive. Recognition that race matters for life experiences and the inclusion of more people seems better than minimizing race altogether. Yet, as I show from the story of pastor Jorge Morales and others in this study, the shift is just that, a shift and not a fix. Disadvantage does not abate with adherence to diversity ideology, it just changes. In other words, being pro-diversity is not the same as being antiracist, or actively opposing racial inequality. The central feature creating continuing disadvantage is commodification. Because diversity displays require that the racial identity of people of color be commodified, employees of color become valuable objects for their respective organizations rather than valuable people. This objectification uses employees of color to satisfy their organizations' need for quantitative diversity.[32] So, what does this mean for how we look at the experiences of employees of color in organizations? Because of commodification, diversity practices can constitute processes of marginalization rather than ameliorate them.

The continuation of racial disadvantage in moving from colorblindness to diversity is due to both ideologies' embeddedness with neoliberalism. Within neoliberalism, the free market is seen as the best arbiter and determinant of value.[33] This rationale mutes conversations about race by claiming a colorblind market, and if the market is colorblind, then it makes no sense to interfere with it to remove racial disadvantage. Simultaneously, neoliberal ideals allow economic value to be derived from racial diversity by turning people's attributes into marketable possessions. Under neoliberalism, all interactions become transactions, so human capacity is valued primarily in dollar terms and auctioned to the highest bidder. As sociologist James Thomas shows in his study of university diversity initiatives, commodified human economic value becomes the justification for diversity initiatives, diverting attention away from equity concerns.[34] The "economization of diversity" thereby allows white people and institutions to increase their value through appeals to diversity without any risk to their position atop the racial hierarchy.

With its connection to neoliberalism, diversity ideology's racially harmful impacts occur on multiple levels. On the macro level, a neoliberal market mentality reinforces the idea that people are to be considered in economic terms, making objectification around racial identity a taken-for-granted idea. On the meso level, organizations create workplace diversity programs that focus on the economic value to the firm that diversity can bring. As a result, firms court external rather than internal legitimacy. On a micro level, whites are free to assume employees of color are present solely to benefit whites. Even personal legitimacy is threatened as employees of color come to question their own qualifications because of the language of diversity.

When neoliberal ideas are taken for granted, there is no room on any level for the recognition of racial inequality, a recognition that is necessary to create solutions focused on equity for employees of color. This is true of both colorblindness, which renders employees of color and their concerns invisible, and diversity ideology, which makes racial identity hypervisible while rendering practically invisible the people carrying those identities. These divergent paths to continuing disadvantage for employees show that the only way to focus on racial inequality is to focus on racial inequality. Neither racial neutrality under colorblindness, nor a focus on how diversity benefits everyone, can prompt the necessary solutions.

Presently, colorblind racism and diversity ideology coexist, with organizations following the logics of one or the other. Because of continuing polarization, I expect this concurrence to continue, but with increasing focus on diversity ideology. As a case in point, sociologists Frank Dobbin and Alexandra Kalev find that hiring for diversity jobs doubled during the period between 2016 and the 2020 murder of George Floyd and then doubled again during the protests following that murder.[35] Although those jobs and related commitments have been clawed back, it remains true that diversity ideology provides the handy benefit of appearing to combat racism in ways that colorblindness does not. As such, even if diversity, equity, and inclusion initiatives are vilified in certain quarters, the need to use people of color to legitimate organizations, activities, and viewpoints will only continue to increase.

Gendered Commodification

Although gender was not the focus of my conversations with women of color, these employees brought up, unprompted, the ways gender intersects with race to create a thoroughgoing experience of commodification. For professors of color, they most often reported their gender further exacerbating the heavy work demands they already face. Women of color have been called the "maids of academe" because of the heavy service and teaching demands placed on them relative to their male counterparts.[36] A Black midwestern professor at a research-intensive university lamented, "I'm very conscious of the fact that women, especially women of color, are asked to do more service compared to their white male counterparts. And that's something that time and time again, we see is something that diminishes the chances of getting tenure." This sentiment was pervasive and echoed by a Latina professor in the Southwest: "Because obviously there is an inequity within the tenure track with women doing more of the service work." When women of color do more service and teaching work, it takes away time for research, which is critical to receiving tenure at many universities.

Women of color were also more subject to threatened personal legitimacy. Gendered racism subjects women of color to an outsider status that pervades the workplace and can undermine their confidence through constant slights and exclusions.[37] Public scholars like sociologist Tressie McMillian Cottom have written about the constant challenges they receive to their credentials and affiliation.[38] These challenges can be exacerbated in environments where both gender and racial diversity are valuable. Women of color are made to feel as though they are a two-fer, hired to meet both racial and gender diversity goals. For example, an Asian American professor in the South was socializing with a white male counterpart when he attacked both her racial and gender identities as the reason that she was hired. "And so I had people over for drinks one day, like the junior faculty in the department, and he goes off on this rant, while drinking my liquor, about how women and minorities are like handed faculty positions, how the system is stacked against white men, and how we were just token hires." This professor experienced an assault on two aspects of her identity in her own home.

The effects of gender on commodification are one place where religious organizations may differ significantly from universities and corporations. Some religious organizations, particularly conservative Protestant churches, have come to value racial diversity, but not gender diversity. Churches with more conservative theology that begin to focus on racial diversity actually have more inequitable environments for women than churches that do not consider race.[39] It is as though churches can do one or the other, but rarely both. This brings about a dilemma when desired racial diversity presents itself in a female body. Women of color serving at these churches experience a high level of subjugated identity. Subjugated identity limits employees of color to the aspects of themselves that are valued by their workplace. When race is valued, but gender is not, it is as if these women are asked to peel themselves apart, representing race but leaving gender behind.

Such was the experience of one Latina pastor in a Southern city. Alejandra Castillo grew up in Central America, the daughter of a diplomat and a pastor. She became acquainted with racial inequality at an early age based on the ways that white missionaries from the United States interacted with her as she translated for their teams. This perspective informs Castillo's work as a theologian, pastor, and educator.

In her second full-time ministry experience, Castillo was recruited as a women's pastor for a church becoming more racially diverse. She quickly found that she would not be fully welcome, despite the fact that they sought her out for employment. This was made evident by the fact that they changed her role from "women's pastor" to "women's director" before the ink on her contract was dry.

> So, if they were just getting awake to race, they were so dead and asleep and numb to gender. They didn't know what to do with a woman like me. They want parts of me but not the whole of me. And I think that's what we feel as women of color in predominantly white institutions. Don't bring all of you. Don't bring all of your experience. Don't bring all of your gender. Just parts of you.

Although the church's desire for diversity opened an opportunity for Castillo to be hired, she was only desired to speak as a person of color, never a Latina. This painful experience gave her a dim perspective of diverse churches. "You want me to help slay racism, but you're not willing to help slay this other system that's also oppressing me? I say that racism and sexism intersectionality is like when you have a baby, and they have a double ear infection. It would be ridiculous to only put antibiotic drops in one ear and not the other." Unless gender diversity became valuable to this church as a way to attract members, it is unlikely they will come to see sexism as a malady worth treating.

Ideologies of Inequality

Instead of giving freedom for employees of color to be themselves, the drive for diversity prompts a display of racial identity within prescribed limits. These limits are circumscribed by which identities can be commodified. Employees of color have to display enough of their racial identity to meet the organization's need for diversity. Only the parts of their identity that benefit the organization are valued, such as in the case of bifurcation of race and gender by women of color. Employees of color must represent this racial identity while not slipping outside of the limits of ethnicity comfortable for whites in the organization. One Latino assistant professor exemplified this balancing act in his recruiting process. First, he had to be a fully identifiable Latino to visibly represent diversity for the university: "I remember folks [on a job board] said that you basically have to play Conga drums, or you have to you have to go in full Ricky Ricardo Conga drum attire to your job talk to get the job. So, they were saying that [the hiring committee] specifically wanted someone to that effect." The implication was that candidates not Latino enough to stand out as a person of color would not be hired.

This same professor who had to be Latino enough to get the job also had to prove his acceptability as a serious colleague since the very Latinidad that made him especially desirable as a candidate threatened to undermine his acceptability in the eyes of his colleagues. He was taken out to lunch with other professors and had to reassure them of how he would perform: "I talked about identity, specifically toward Latinos. And it got kind of like a kind of a tepid response. But, as soon as I focused on submitting to particular journals or presenting at particular conferences or doing that kind of like checking those boxes, they were really happy." This professor had to prove himself separately as an obvious Latino and as a serious scholar. The subjugated identity that resulted made him think of his Latinidad and his academic pursuits as two separated identities, alternatively required by his employer in different situations. "I felt like I had to craft sort of a double identity. And I'm able to speak to my Latino identity and my identity as a scholar. So, just like I speak Spanish fluently, and I literally think in Spanish and English, I feel like I have like a double kind of identity that way." There was no room in his workplace for a Latino scholar, only a Latino and a scholar.

Commodification under diversity ideology takes an element of an employee's identity, makes it visible, and capitalizes on it. The ways that this happens, like being used in a diversity photo, may seem a minor inconvenience. But the sum of these daily experiences amounts to dehumanization. Employees of color come to recognize that their ability to represent diversity is seen as more valuable than they are, especially when inconvenient aspects of their identity are discarded.

At this point, the cynical reader might be thinking, "Well, isn't having a job enough?" That is to say, are these experiences really worth critiquing, given how hard it is to get these jobs in the first place? It is true that without the push to bring in employees of color that diversity ideology prompts, they might not be hired at all because of discrimination that stands in the way.[40] The simple answer to whether having a job is enough: it depends on what the goal is. Higher levels of employment for people of color, especially in managerial jobs such as the ones described in this study, could theoretically help narrow the racial gap in employment levels and income. But if the goal is to close the gap rather than narrow it, that is not possible while employees of color experience more detrimental work conditions than whites. The employees I spoke with experience fewer opportunities for advancement and more threats to well-being that limit career longevity. These costs are incredibly harmful to employees of color. Studies show that long-term experience in jobs with low satisfaction is no better for life satisfaction than unemployment.[41] I can only conclude that if the goal is racial equity, no, just having a job is not enough. The jobs of employees of color must offer an experience equitable to those of whites in the same positions.

3 One of the Things about Bridges Is They Get Walked On

One Sunday morning, Pastor Duncan Unger was suddenly incapacitated as he stood in the pulpit. Although he recognized the words on the notes in front of him, they were stuck somewhere between his mind and his mouth: "We are talking ten plus minutes this is going on. My wife got ladies in the church and ran out in the hallway. It was visibly just too scary [for her]. And I look at my notes, and I understood every word, sentence structure, paragraph. I just could not move it from the paper to the congregation."

Unger sought a diagnosis to explain what happened to him that day. After an MRI and blood tests to rule out a stroke or Lyme disease, doctors told him there was nothing physically wrong. Finally, he found himself in a counselor's office. Only after the counselor probed what Unger did for a living did the pastor receive a diagnosis. The counselor's assessment included a revelation about the stress Unger had been living under at work.

I did not know how unhealthy I was until I was diagnosed. I was having neurological problems, loss of balance, memory issues, substituted words for other words. I began to have massive headaches. I went to a counselor, and he said to me, this is chronic stress. So, chronic stress is not event-based. It's years of your stress hormones being always on and feeling out of control, and that you have no way out. It is always a fight and flight. It is always constant anxiety. And when he said that, I realized for a good while I had been living every day anxious, worried about what was going to happen.

When we spoke, Pastor Unger pinpointed the cause of his stress, and it was not the day-in, day-out burdens of being a religious leader. Rather, it was directly connected to his position as a pastor of color in a diverse church. Because of his church's efforts to be seen as diverse by hiring him, Pastor Unger became the victim of congregational backlash that threatened his personal legitimacy. The feeling of not being accepted or respected by congregants wore on him over time. In addition, Pastor Unger experienced limited social support, since the other pastors neither shared in this stress nor provided him any resources to better deal with it. Pastor Unger remembered in detail the disgruntled letter written by former church members that started his growing discomfort. "They [the former church members] called us things like an 'affirmative action church,' which was really hurtful to me. Especially since out of twenty people hired since the beginning of the church, I was the only minority. Townhall meetings were had, emails were sent. It was really just bad; it was hurtful."

From the time of this conflict, the church became a place of attack rather than solace for Pastor Unger. His confidence was shaken, and he found himself unable to do relatively simple aspects of his job.

I didn't want to stand in the pulpit. I didn't want to be there. I didn't feel all the way protected. I began to cocoon and isolate myself. And only had a few friends that I would hang around, and I just began to shut down. It took my sense of well-being. My sense of safety. Standing in the pulpit was difficult. Just for announcements, to do an announcement because you don't know when you're standing in a place that could be hostile.

Pastor Unger was the target of hostility related to "affirmative action" and the rest of the church staff left him to bear that burden alone. As a result, he became increasingly unable to do his job and subject to health concerns. Had the church staff supported him as the church diversified, the results may have been different. As it was, the church did not give Unger resources for the position they put him in.

Stress from work situations is not uncommon and has negative effects, including greater anxiety and job dissatisfaction.[1] When employees of color take on roles in organizations working to be diverse, they are at higher risk for stress at work. As discussed in the previous chapter, organizations attempting to show themselves as diverse often engage in commodification of employees of color. This commodification results in high job demands, threats to legitimacy, and subjugated identity; the perfect recipe for stress related to the workplace. In the present chapter, I will return to these outcomes of commodification. By revisiting high job demands, threats to legitimacy, and subjugated identity here, I will show that they not only occur among employees of color in diverse workplaces but also that each of outcomes is linked to emotional and physical concerns for employees of color. These physical and emotional consequences, ranging from stroke-like symptoms in Pastor Unger's case to depression and insomnia in others, are remarkably common and devastating for the lives of employees I spoke with.

Job Strain

Employees who are forced to be representatives of their groups pay for it with their "energy, resources, labor, time, and health."[2] In addition, interactions across racial groups in diverse spaces can create stress. Finally, employees of color may have difficulty meeting the expectations of race-related labor and the core expectations of their job simultaneously. For these employees, their disadvantaged position in the racial structure gives them less latitude to negotiate conflicting expectations.[3]

What social scientists call "job strain" occurs when high levels of demand meet low levels of autonomy in an environment of limited social support. Experiencing job strain has been associated with physical health concerns, depression, insomnia, work-family conflict, emotional exhaustion, and psychological distress.[4] Employees of color experience higher job strain compared to other workers. Interestingly, this higher level of job strain occurs despite the fact that employees of color are *no more likely* to occupy high-strain occupations.[5] So, it is not so much the jobs themselves generating job strain but that employees of color have qualitatively different experiences in job than their white counterparts.

The vast majority of the employees I spoke with noted one or more physical or emotional symptoms or health incidents that they directly related to their position at work in a diverse organization. Although I did not expressly recruit for employees experiencing stress or strain at work, forty-nine of the sixty employees in this study mentioned these sorts of harms with varying levels of severity. These employees also witnessed the damage done to those around them. For example, one Black assistant professor, when asked what work to uphold diversity costs employees of color, noted:

I mean, it's a high cost for Black women. There are so many Black women in academia who are sick. They're physically sick. Some people have passed earlier than they should have passed from this stress. And I think that one of the things that I have learned in my time as faculty, just watching how white women move and some Latinas move too, is that they will talk about their stress. They'll say, "Look, I got two kids at home, I got one on the way, my husband's this, my granny's that." They have seventy-five reasons as to why they can't do something because they're so stressed. And I think that Black women are so accustomed to just doing a lot that sometimes we don't pump the brakes on ourselves, and if you don't pump the brakes on the institution, they're gonna suck the life out of you. And so, I think that there's a sense of there's something we feel like we have to prove but then I also feel like the institutions exploit us and they don't provide much in return. And they see us as disposable. So, I think it's a really high cost.

This statement of the burdens borne by Black women in academia includes overwork and struggle for personal legitimacy. This professor has seen how both heavy work demands and the need to prove belonging in the face of threats to legitimacy result in undue amounts of stress. She connects the stress to Black women's work choices in combination with exploitation by the university. This statement reflects not only what she sees in her counterparts but also what she has experienced herself. When speaking of the stress she is subject to in the academy, she says, "It's debilitating." She projects that, after years of being part of the academic system, she will experience chronic illness or even early death. The untimely deaths of Black women academics underscore the grim reality of her projection.[6]

The negative experiences of employees of color in management-level jobs have often been attributed to discrimination; I posit that job strain for this group may be *more specifically an outcome of commodification.*[7] While the employees I spoke with point to instances of discrimination, those are not what they name as the genesis of their stress. In conversation, the aspects of commodification came up again and again in conjunction with the physical and emotional symptoms noted by employees of color. Recall that commodification here includes the objectification of employees of color for the benefit of others as well as how others react to employees of color because they have been made symbols of diversity. Because commodification and its effects create job strain, current diversity practices and the ideology informing them create bad jobs for employees of color, lowering job satisfaction.

Heavy Work Demands

One way commodification can result in heavy work demands is in the amount of work relative to the results garnered. Here, employees of color are disadvantaged by being given the responsibility to make changes in the racial environment of their organizations but insufficient power to do so. Sociologist Adia Harvey Wingfield refers to this as racial outsourcing.[8] In her study, employees from technicians to doctors are charged with improving the racial climate for patients and other employees. The only qualification they have for this work is their racial identity. When their sense of responsibility for racial issues meets a relative lack of authority, frustration and work dissatisfaction follows. The disconnect between responsibility and authority creates job strain.

One case of this is a Black pastor in California. Darrell Winston had a dual role, working as a minister within his church and in his denomination office. For the denomination, he had the responsibility of helping them become more demographically diverse by recruiting African American pastors. During Winston's tenure, the number of Black pastors in his denomination increased from twelve to over two hundred. Having succeeded at that task, he wanted to change to a new focus, creating healthier instead of more diverse churches. He told me, "The denomination's model then was multiplying healthy churches among all people. So, I was part of the 'all people' part. I wanted to move to more of the 'healthy churches' part." Not only was he not able to make that transition, but he was also fired from his position after attempting to shift focus.

When I asked Pastor Winston what trying to promote diversity in the church had cost him, he spoke directly about the mismatch between responsibility and authority. "Most of my trauma has been with relationships that included deep betrayal, tokenism, where I was the only one expected to do [diversity work], had lots of responsibility but no authority, and having to carry all of that. Being expected to make change, but there's not really a commitment to change." Although Pastor Winston's primary role was related to recruiting Black pastors, as the one Black denominational employee, he had all things racial put on his shoulders. He managed to succeed despite rather than because of his role, citing limited authority to do what he was asked to accomplish.

Having the weight of improving the denomination's racial climate without the resources to accomplish the work left Pastor Winston with lasting health concerns that he tie back to the stress of his position at work.

I carried my stress physically for years. On top of that, unbeknownst to me, I had a condition called Cushing's disease. I had a small tumor on my pituitary gland. And it's acting as a stress hormone disease. So, it's like the worst condition to have in this line of work. So, all the stress that I've been experiencing was being magnified inside my body. I had the tumor removed. Praise God; I'm cured. But the scars remain. Yeah, lot of scars for me that I experienced. Sleep apnea, diabetes, tumors, and kidney stones. That's what my body went through.

As a representative of diversity, Pastor Winston experienced a physical toll to his health through the heavy work burdens laid on him. He was then unceremoniously fired once he no longer desired to do diversity work. It took Pastor Winston five years to find a position not related to diversity in another organization, highlighting how such positions can limit career mobility.

Another example of the heavy job demands created from responsibility without authority comes from an Asian American pastor who took on the weight of creating change within his church. For two years, he served as de facto interim lead pastor of his church without ever officially being named to the role. Despite his lack of title, he successfully stewarded the church to record giving and attendance levels. In the end, however, he still was not given the job to lead his church permanently. The church hired a white lead pastor well-known for his writings on diversity instead. The Asian American pastor expressed regret over what he had given to the church without receiving what he needed in return. "I'm taking these blows for this mission, trying to push forward diversity, race, helping people understand and see different perspectives and even broaden theologies, but I don't think I took care of myself." He lamented his exhaustion and openly wondered, "What does it actually mean to be the token, versus actually being empowered?"

High job demands also arise as employees of color support constituencies of color on top of their work responsibilities. This work is often uncompensated and unrecognized. One Latino assistant professor decided to catalog his work demands in hopes of some additional compensation. "I took that to the dean, and I said, 'Hey look, this semester, I spent thirty hours supporting marginalized students. When you decide how much raise I should get, I think you should take that into account.' I think because my other colleagues do have that extra time to write papers, that I should be compensated somehow." While he did not receive a raise, he did receive an award. His excitement about it was lukewarm at best: "Yes. I was very happy to get an award. But that's just like a pat on the back."

Another employee who faced high work demands in racialized labor for constituencies of color was employed at a hospital system located in a majority Black area. Jamie Bixner is a Black PR professional who formerly worked as a news reporter. Although it was not part of her job responsibilities, Bixner was pressed into service to create video messages for her hospital. This new work came after a consultant suggested posting messages about the hospital designed to endear it to the surrounding community, even as the hospital expanded and further inconvenienced residents. When I asked her why she was taking on work outside her role, Bixner replied, "Well, actually an outside consultant said I would be great to communicate these messages to our target audience. We've had sort of a rocky relationship with the residents of the city because we've been building."

Bixner herself had not reflected on the additional work this new position placed on her as well as the potential connection to her racial identity. For example, when I asked Bixner whether she had received any additional pay for the work she was doing, or even if it was made part of her official job responsibilities, she seemed taken aback, as though it had not occurred to her that these things should happen. She laughingly replied, "You're right; I did not get extra pay for that." Although Bixner admitted that she was specifically brought to the all-white team by PR consultants seeking to reach a Black community, she hadn't explicitly thought that it might have something to do with her race. "So, I don't know . . . I'm not technically on the team, but I probably have as much or more experience than most people. So, that's been hard for me to distinguish whether it's a race thing, because there were, there are no African Americans on the marketing team."

Although she has doubts, it seems likely that Bixner was pressed into service as a Black ambassador to a majority Black community for no additional recognition or pay. She has not even been made an official part of the team that she now regularly does work for.

Internal and Personal Legitimacy

Bixner's role in creating PR videos for the surrounding community also comes with consequences for internal legitimacy. Recall, internal legitimacy is threatened when employees question the rightness of their employers, and by extension, their own actions.[9] Being confronted with the disconnect between organizational promises and realities, and then having to defend their organizations' external marketing, creates stress and cognitive dissonance within employees of color. In Bixner's case, the struggle for internal legitimacy manifests in decoupling between the hospital's image externally and the hospital's internal activities. Although the hospital had a paucity of high-ranking Black employees, Bixner pulled them into her videos over and over. When I jokingly asked if she put the same doctor in the videos every time, I found that she had been doing just that!

> There was one who was particularly community oriented. So, we used him a lot because he was just a young, good-looking guy. We wanted to use him a lot, but then he wanted to be involved a lot. But he's at another hospital now, so there's not that guy anymore. There are a couple of women that we use a lot. They got a little irritated, like they're tired of being used to put up there. But they're good-looking women, very smart, and African American, so we want to use them. Some people get tired of being used in that way

because they know what's going on. I can understand [the irritation], but I still want them to participate because we need that balance. We need that face. We need that profile of the doctor who's super smart, super articulate. We need that image.

Bixner's efforts to portray a certain image of the hospital eventually met with aggravation as the same people were used again and again to make inroads with the community. Bixner continues to actively reproduce this problem for her fellow employees despite her awareness of their discomfort. The language Bixner used here clearly exhibits commodification: we *use* these employees for what we *need*.

Although Bixner is zealous in producing diversity displays for the hospital, she was not completely unconflicted. Toward the end of our time together, I asked her what effect portraying the hospital in this positive light might have. Her response automatically went to ideas of guilt, even though I did not present the question in that way: "I think that I see what they're trying to do, so I don't feel bad about portraying them in that way. And I just hope that then it gets there, and I think it will. So yeah, I don't feel bad. Is that what you asked me? If I felt bad?" I did not ask her if she felt bad, but that was the question Bixner felt compelled to answer.

While Bixner only had a twinge of guilt about her work on diversity displays, threats to organizational legitimacy had more pronounced effects for others. Bryce Rhodes is a Black pastoral resident hired by a large Southern church. The church took a great deal of pride in its status as multiethnic, especially given the racial divisions of the city where it sits. The heavy workload demanded by this church took a toll on everyone: "Yeah, you were stressed because they had a saying [about the pastors]—they are thoroughbreds and we let them run—it was high paced. I drank more coffee than I ever drank before. I think I was just really, really stressed out. Because you got to keep up with everything. So that's how it manifests itself. So, headaches, all that kind of stuff."

But it wasn't so much the stressful schedule that Rhodes paid for the most. Even more so than the workload, what affected him and the other Black pastoral residents was the difference between the image that the church portrayed and what went on behind the scenes. Because of the scars from his experience at this diverse church, Rhodes struggles with disillusionment and wouldn't advise other pastors of color to work at a similar church without serious reflection. The idea of counting the costs is another way of saying: Do not start something unless you have the resources you need to finish.[10] Rhodes states that tremendous inner resources are needed to survive / thrive for pastors of color in a diverse environment. His description of the pressure that employees of color bear is so apt it inspired the title of this chapter.

> You gotta learn how to be a bridge-builder, but one of the things about bridges is they get walked on. Count the costs. Do due diligence. Do they want some token, or are they serious? If you have a family, count the cost on your kids, wife, you will be pulled in a lot of different directions and there are gonna be a lot of sleepless nights and a lot of teary nights and a lot of times where you live in this constant state of disappointment. You have the expectation of you wanting to see this amazing utopian experience, right? But the reality sets in, and you're going to be right in the middle. In counting the costs, you're going to have to come to grips with being acquainted with disappointment. The forgiveness that you're going to have to extend is not going to be enough. You need to have utter total dependence on God.

Here, Rhodes calls being a pastor of color in a multiracial church something so hard that only God could accomplish it. The difference between the promise of being part of a diverse organization and the reality of it is what burdens Rhodes, and not him alone but also his entire family. This loss of internal legitimacy is not something Rhodes can just distance himself from; because of what he has given up to be part of this church, he feels himself to be right in the middle of it.

Threats to legitimacy and the costs thereof also happen at the personal level. Employees of color experienced harms from the constant slights that cause them to doubt themselves, as they are characterized as "diversity hires." The pressure to prove that they belong creates tremendous stress for employees of color. When asked to name his primary source of stress as an assistant professor, a Latino from the West Coast went directly to this idea of having to prove himself. "There's definitely stress," he replied. "Going through the interview process, and even now as faculty, I personally feel the need to disprove the belief that I'm a minority hire or that I was being interviewed because of my minority status. I feel the need to show that I am deserving, capable, my science is good. And I'm not a diversity hire."

The pressure to defend oneself against assumptions spoken and unspoken about their competence required additional emotional and mental resources from employees of color that their colleagues did not have to expend. A Black corporate employee expressed that even being great isn't enough. She feels pressure to be the best of the best. "There's also the stress of whatever you do, you gotta be top top. Gotta be top top. Like you always need to be going above and beyond." The commodification of diversity that shone a spotlight on employees of color also cast them in a subordinate position, feeling as though they had to defend their work even to peers at their level.

Subjugated Identity

Employees of color lost their sense of identity as they were "othered." They were not able to enact their preferred identity and instead had to comport themselves in the manner preferred by their work context. Commodification turns employees of color into objects for the benefit of their organizations. bell hooks aptly captures how this objectification limits agency: "As objects, one's reality is defined by others, one's identity is created by others."[11] Therefore, employees of color are not free to chart their own path but only to exist in a narrow space defined by others. This restriction pigeonholes employees of color by setting them in opposition to the dominant group within their workplaces. Commodification under diversity ideology requires this othering to determine who is us and who is them, and what the value of "them" is.[12] Employees of color are not free to be who they are but only a representative of their group, and lack the agency needed to set their own group boundaries.[13] This becomes even more harmful when they are lumped into a group that is not their own.

An example of this is Alan Wah, a pastor on the East Coast. As a second-generation Chinese immigrant, he served as the bridge between an American and Chinese congregation for years after they merged. While he was faithfully committed to that role, he paid a tremendous personal cost. First of all, he felt the intense stress of being the one in the middle; he believed if he did not play this role that the entire merger might collapse. "Yeah, I was the critical bridge between the two churches to make this relationship work. That probably added to my sense of stress and almost burn-out at that church. I wasn't sleeping very well. And then I start, I just felt really stuck, like I had to be the one to make things work, which is unhealthy."

In addition to the stress of being caught in the middle, Wah experienced costs to his identity. Wah is Cantonese speaking but was bridging for a majority Mandarin-speaking congregation. Because of his role, he lost time to invest in his own cultural herit-age and pass that along to his children. This became a source of regret over his time at the church.

> I guess there was a cost in terms of my connection with my family's cultural background because you only have so much time to split. My family is Cantonese, and the church is not Cantonese; it is mostly mainland Chinese Mandarin speaking. So, if you want to preserve your sense of connection and pass that on to your chil-dren, I would say that I lost that. You only have so much energy, and mine was spent in translating the Mandarin church in expres-sion. So, it's a matter of how much you can invest in each of your cultural influences and associations.

The loss of his Cantonese heritage was a struggle Wah navigated alone. The white congregants he was translating for did not even notice he was going beyond his own culture to make things easier for them. "Because they would just see Chinese," Wah reported.

Wah was not alone in having to bridge between white congre-gants or leadership to a group that was not his own. I also spoke to Venezuelan pastors doing their best to bridge between white and majority Mexican congregations, African American pastors trying to connect Nigerian congregations, and Korean pastors trying to be a bridge for every single immigrant in their church. In these cases, the narrowness of identity allowed to these leaders added to stress and struggles in their role. While "being the bridge" is a common analogy used for bringing together different racial/ethnic groups, it was not a positive phrase for many employees in my sample because of the objectification and inability to be oneself that the bridging role brought about. As one Black pastor said, quoting public theologian Ekemini Uwan, "But the blood of Jesus is your bridge, not my back."[14]

Being subject to objectification does not just affect the employees themselves; it also affects their families. I spoke to one Black pastor from a church in the South. Pastor James Johnson was brought in by a white pastoral couple leading a church in a majority Black area. Only after coming to the church did he find out that he was hired just after the lead pastor was accused of racism. As I will discuss in the next chapter, being brought in after an accusation of racism was experienced almost exclusively by Black employees. While his boss was not forthcoming with information about the accusations, congregants let him know about the history after he arrived. Johnson felt he was able to make an impact through the work he was doing, but he was frustrated that his primary value to the organization seemed to come from his race rather than his abilities. During our interview, he let out a big sigh. When I asked him what it was about, I received this response:

> From the standpoint of being a Black man on this team and knowing that I've been brought in to make the picture, right? It didn't feel great. Didn't feel great. I started graying. I did. I mean, I saw more gray hair sprout out than at any other point in my life. I was constantly tired. And so, this stuff is just hard. It's just tough. And I just find myself exhausted. That's what that big sigh was.

As our conversation continued, Pastor Johnson began to talk about some aspects of his stress that affected his family relationships. Job stresses frequently seep into the home, affecting familial harmony.[15] Because of Pastor Johnson's work stress, he caused his wife anxiety and was curt with his kids. He explained to me that although he has tried to refrain from talking about his job strain at home, it still shows up in his house. "It just comes out in other unhealthy ways. I find myself being short with my kids. They're just little kids. The stress of that environment, I bring that home and it manifests itself in being drained and being depressed and not being 100 percent to my family." As with comedian Chris Rock's statement in the epigraph to this chapter, Pastor Johnson discovered that what was best for his own children was not necessarily compatible with integration into a majority white space.[16]

Without even knowing, Pastor Johnson took on the role of "Black pastor" in a church that desperately needed one. He and his family have paid the price in terms of stress and strained dynamics. Being subject to this objectification also diminishes Pastor Johnson's value as a minister. "I don't feel seen," he lamented. "It's one thing when you value what I bring to the table because I'm a qualified, skilled individual. It's another thing when it suits your need for a token."

Another Black pastor also spoke to what being objectified did to him. He saw himself as a trophy for his organization more than a member of the clergy. "I was just a trinket, a trophy on a shelf. It broke me and made me really bitter and resentful. And every now and then [leadership would say], 'Oh, let me look at my trophy that gets me points with young Black people, let me go dust him off.' So, I just felt isolated, I felt used, ignored, manipulated." He felt his presence was nothing more than a ploy to gain the church young,

Black congregants. When he was not actively playing that role, he felt "not heard."

Employees of color also pay for the efforts they must make to reject controlling images. Controlling images dehumanize subordinated groups by subjecting them to negative portrayals that they have to combat.[17] Coined initially to explore the constrained roles that Black women find themselves in, such as mammies or jezebels, this concept has broad utility in the lives of employees of color. Employees I spoke with noted the physical and emotional harms caused by having to fight others' ideas of who they should be. Having to push back on controlling images limits employees of color's space for action within their organizations.

One example is how employees of color try to be the professionally "acceptable" sort of people from their group. This requires careful cultivation of one's image and manners of speech to avoid rejection. Even one's facial expression must be controlled. One Black assistant professor, speaking about the additional calculations she needs to make even in casual conversation, explained, "That's how I have to be on campus. I have to think through conversations with everyone. Okay, what if someone says this? How am I going to make sure I don't make a crazy-ass face back to them? How can I explain this? What literature do I need to bring with me, all of that stuff?"

Another Black assistant professor touted her acceptability as a likely component of her hiring. "Being a person of color that's nonthreatening. I see myself, and I think people probably read me as a safe kind of person of color because I'm biracial and speak with a certain class privilege. And there's a certain kind of presentation of self I think you need to have. You can't be too radical. You can talk about race, but you can't really talk about Blackness." In applying for a job that explicitly mentioned how great the surrounding community was for Black families, this professor observed and absorbed what was seen as being Black enough to check the diversity box but not so much to threaten white sensibilities. As legal scholar Nancy Leong puts it, this professor must be "identifiably nonwhite to benefit from their nonwhiteness, yet the version of nonwhiteness they perform must meet with white approval."[18] Diverse others, particularly racial minorities, add spice to life via their food, dress, and other customs but are otherwise expected to adhere to normative standards of behavior and are assumed to have normative (read white) experiences. When they fail to do so, diverse organizations lose their appeal.[19] This professor could be herself to the extent that she fit the presentation of self that was desired by her employer. The portions that deviated, she was encouraged to hide.

An Asian American professor at a Southern university also felt like she had to mold herself and scholarship into an acceptable template to be successful in her role. This stressed her mental health in a way that goes above the normal stress generated within academia. She explained, "I get that everybody struggles with mental health, but it's also because of a white culture of academia and colonial culture of, 'You have to write this way. You have to produce knowledge in that way.' I'm going to the doctor next week because I've had a lot of stomach issues lately, and my counselor thinks it's because of all the built-up stress and anxiety." The stress of fitting a white cultured way of doing things on top of the already potent pressures of an academic job created physical pain for this professor that was left to be addressed in the doctor's and counselor's offices. The fact that her additional stresses as a woman of color are dismissed as just part of doing the work only adds to what she is experiencing.

As seen in chapter 2, when used as objects by their diverse organizations, employees of color experience commodification that creates heavy job demands, threats to internal organizational and personal legitimacy, and subjugated identity. In this chapter, I have shown examples of how these three outcomes of commodification affect physical and emotional well-being. Work/family conflict, insomnia, chronic stress, health concerns, and other symptoms were frequently reported by employees who I talked with. Each attributed their experiences in some way to their commoditized presence within a diverse workplace.

The enactment of diversity ideology creates the conditions for job strain, even in jobs that should be high quality. Diversity ideology offers the push to bring in more employees of color, but because the emphasis is on organizational benefits and not the health of the employees, the latter gets largely ignored. Employees of color are brought into positions that simply demand more of them than their white counterparts. They pay the costs with their health and well-being.

Many diversity initiatives focus on the recruitment and retention of employees of color at management levels. A common frustration within companies is that there is much higher attrition among employees of color in contrast to their white peers, creating the pressure to recruit more and more people of color. It has long been known that job strain creates excess turnover.[20] It is ironic then that perhaps the same ideology promoting numerical diversity may create the conditions that threaten it. Diversity ideology undergirds practices that commodify employees of color, which in turn creates job strain for these employees that may shorten their organizational tenure.

Social Support

Great coworkers can help moderate job strain through social support. But employees of color who I spoke with did not feel social support from their coworkers, nor did they feel that their coworkers understood what they were going through. Social support can be broadly grouped into two major types. Affective support happens when people feel cared about as individuals and are able to connect with their coworkers, like having people join for happy hour after work. Instrumental support consists of tangible support getting the work done, such as sharing data or best practices.[21] Not having either can be incredibly detrimental to employees. One Black assistant professor at an elite liberal arts school described how pressure to be the best, combined with social isolation, made it difficult to complete even mundane tasks.

I've never been clinically diagnosed, but I'm almost positive I have a form of anxiety. Because of all this. I often feel tightness in my chest, or butterflies in my stomach, like a nervousness almost. Anytime I get an email from work, anytime I check my email, I get tensed up to the point where I've been paralyzed from doing a lot of stuff in the last few months. Things I used to be able to rally to do, like, I could just sit down and do a lesson plan, now it incapacitates me to do it. That is probably the fact that I don't feel comfortable at work. I didn't realize a lot of that had to do with the people I work with. In my own department, I'd go weeks, and no one would say anything to me. I was on the second floor, right by the stairs, so they had to go by my office to go to their offices, and no one would say anything to me. I internalize that because I'm a very,

very outgoing person. And I internalize it to be like, "Okay, what am I doing wrong? Am I playing my music too loud?" I didn't realize until about maybe a year and a half into the job that all that stuff was connected, and it was making me physically sick. So yeah, there definitely have been some physical and mental hurdles in terms of feeling exhausted.

This professor is already under a great deal of stress to prove himself in academia. When his coworkers ignore him, he blames himself and his symptoms worsen. In a similar fashion, a West Coast assistant professor experienced physical symptoms from lack of social support. These symptoms manifested when she had plans with coworkers canceled again and again. Feeling rejected exacerbated her stress. "They're like, 'Oh, yeah, let's go see Ali Wong; let's go see a concert.' But then, all of a sudden, nobody could make it. And at first, it's hurtful, because it's like, I'm trying, but they don't really want to be in my presence. I think it manifests in my body in weird ways. Like, it'll impact my sleep or my eyes start to twitch if I feel stressed out."

While this professor recounts the serious consequences of lack of social support, she acknowledges her job has a number of advantages compared to other forms of employment. As a professor, she has a great deal of latitude when determining how to do her job, which hours to be in the office, and the like. She offers a caveat to her account of stress by saying, "But it's also not the end of the world, right? It's not like I have colleagues busting down my door telling me what to do or how to do it. It's just the sense of like, I'm different, and I need to just be okay with that and not feel that anything will be different in terms of the Black-white divide."

This professor's description of workplace freedom acknowledges her autonomy at work—a factor highly correlated with job satisfaction. Being able to control one's own work is associated with low levels of physical symptoms and role stress.[22] But, although she has tremendous autonomy, she still experiences job stress, worsened by a lack of social support that manifests in physical symptoms. In the face of rejection from her coworkers, this professor retreats into social networks with other professionals of color: "I just try to work out and I try to build my community outside of my institution. That's my safe space."

Differences in Job Strain by Organization Type

In her book *The Trouble with Passion*, sociologist Erin Cech investigates the issues that arise from making work integral to one's identity.[23] I echo those findings here. While most employees of color I spoke with show some signs of distress, those whose work was more integral to their lives and identities struggled more. For pastors and professors, fully nine out of ten employees described physical and emotional symptoms of job strain related to their commodification. For corporate employees, while still high, the number was closer to three out of every four. The difference that came up most often in my conversations is the level of job involvement—the degree to which one's job is integrally connected to one's life. "An individual with a high degree of job involvement would place the job at the center of his/her life's interests."[24] Job involvement has positive effects such as improved job satisfaction and organizational attachment, but it is a double-edged sword. Employees with high job involvement experience the effects of job strain more acutely than those less involved with work.

For members of the clergy, their high level of job involvement was revealed in their use of the term "calling." Calling, in the religious sense, has been defined as "that inner persuasion or experience whereby a person feels himself directly summoned or invited by God to take up the work of the ministry."[25] Those who are called feel compelled to their work out of obedience to a higher power. So profound is this sense of calling that it supersedes typical occupational boundaries and spills over into one's life, becoming a central part of their identity. For pastors in this study, calling was salient in explaining why they do the work that they do. Pastor Unger, despite the chronic stress he suffers in his role, used the language of calling to share why he does not regret taking the job. "And I believe totally I'm called. So, I would do it again." Another pastor described her calling this way: "My job is to do the thing God calls me to do, to say the things that God calls me to say, to be in spaces that God calls me to be in, but to trust him to do whatever the work is." Because these clergy see their jobs as a calling, the inability to detach from work and the extent to which work is tied to identity is increased. People with callings struggle to disengage both physically and mentally with work in ways that can be detrimental to health.[26]

For professors, a high level of job involvement is built into the structure of academia. Because jobs in higher education frequently require relocating across the country, assistant professors found themselves living away from family and friend support networks. This relative isolation made work more central to their lives. One professor at a rural Midwestern location told me about the hardship that creates: "Most folks, especially people of color, don't have family around them. So, I think the distance is very draining." Speaking of his personal story leaving family, a Latino professor in the Southwest said, "Because we are academics, there is an element of self-sacrifice. I had to give up any kind of preference over where I wanted to live. It would be great if I could be with my family, and I could be in my community doing this. But I'm not. That's the way academia works." Being detached from community, professors made work a larger part of their lives and hours. One told me that he would "work in the libraries until midnight, so the students can just pop over." The level of sacrifice only heightens the importance of career success.

Whether prompted by calling or by location, job involvement tends to be higher for pastors and professors than for other professionals in this study. This high level of job involvement heightens the effects of job strain, resulting in the physiological responses detailed here. The old adage affirming the effortlessness of meaningful work goes, "If you do what you love, you'll never work a day in your life." For employees of color, this may not be true if their work "loves" them back by objectifying them. The more meaningful and central work was to their lives, the more dangerous the conditions of commodification were to employees of color. What's worse, employees with high levels of job involvement are less likely to detach from their work in the off-hours. This lack of ability to disconnect limited the degree to which employees of color could recover from their daily stress.

Good Jobs to Bad Jobs

In *Good Jobs, Bad Jobs,* sociologist Arne Kalleburg lists among the qualities that make a job "good" high levels of autonomy, flexible schedules, and intrinsic rewards.[27] The jobs of pastor, professor, and professional in this study by and large meet those criteria. In fact, one of the jobs in this study, that of clergy, tops the general social survey as the most satisfying of all jobs. The accounts of employees of color reveal that these features are not enough to compensate for the high job demands, threats to legitimacy, and subjugated identity that result from commodification. What's more, social support, as a key moderator of job strain, is not always readily available to these employees. When employees of color are commodified by their workplaces, they suffer job strain that manifests in physical symptoms, emotional stress, and work/family conflict, turning good jobs into bad ones.

While diversity practices may be effective at bringing employees of color into majority white workplaces, they often fail to keep them. The negative experiences arising from diversity ideology provide a clue as to why. When employees perceive that the diversity initiatives in their workplace do not result in equity for them, they are more likely to leave.[28] These organizational outcomes not only result in expenses for employers; they also leave emotionally and physically harmed employees in their wake. The experiences of these employees of color provide ample evidence that employees cannot thrive while being dehumanized by commodification.

4 Honorary Whites and Collective Blacks

Degrees of Diversity

In the previous three chapters, each of the opening vignettes featured a Black professor, professional, or pastor. Foregrounding the experiences of Black employees is intentional. Although all groups in this study experience remarkable—and remarkably similar—harms arising from how diversity is employed within their workplaces, these harms are not entirely equivalent. In this chapter, I will focus on the nuances between groups, showing how diversity ideology interacts with the racial identities of Asian, Black, and Latino/a employees to exact disparate consequences.[1] I also advance the term *conditional commodification* to discuss how some employees can conditionally opt out of commodification under diversity ideology.

Three primary factors determine the relative costs of diversity ideology to employees of color: whether they are viewed as a representative of diversity; the content of controlling images concerning their group; and the social distance, or the level of understanding and empathy, between their group and whites.[2]

Because of these factors, Black employees bear the highest costs of diversity within the workplace. On the opposite end of the spectrum, Asian employees report a relatively privileged experience. Over half of Black and Latina/o people, and over three-quarters of Asian Americans, see Asian Americans as racially closer to people of color than whites.[3] Despite this closeness, my respondents described Asian Americans as separated from the problems that other people of color face. For example, one Latino professor, when asked about racial representation in his department, replied, "I'm the only faculty of color. There are two assistant or associate professors that are female. One is white, the other was Chinese." Likewise, a South Asian assistant professor explained, "I advocate on behalf of people of color, but not as a person of color. In my mind, I feel like I'm advocating for people of color the way white people advocate for people of color, like, as an ally, as someone who is doing what I think is right and trying to promote a world I want it to be, as opposed to what it currently is." Because of his racialization as Asian, he feels he can distance himself from the issues of people of color and advocate as someone on the outside.

A hierarchy of experiences for employees of color derives in part from the racial hierarchy that exists in the United States. While this hierarchy positions whites in the dominant position, it does not leave people of color as an undifferentiated mass. Sociologist Eduardo Bonilla-Silva suggests three categories in this hierarchy: white, honorary white, and collective Black.[4] In his scheme, the category of whites includes those traditionally considered white, as well as assimilated Latino/as, and urban, assimilated Indigenous people. Collective Blacks include those traditionally considered Black, as well as dark-skinned Latino/as, and Asians such as Vietnamese and Hmong people. Honorary whites fall somewhere in the middle and include most Asians and lighter-complected Latino/as. Examining how diversity ideology's effects interact with racial hierarchy in what follows reveals a degree of resonance with Bonilla-Silva's categories; some nonwhite groups carry a much heavier burden than others.

Conditional Commodification: Asian Experiences

Studies show that Asian Americans experience higher levels of intermarriage with whites, lower residential segregation, and higher incomes.[5] Because of their position as honorary whites, Asian employees reported experiencing the effects of commodification less acutely than Black or Latino/a employees I spoke with. There are a number of reasons why this is the case. The first relates to the impact of racial identity. As discussed previously, being employed in an organization portraying itself as diverse leads to a subjugated identity for employees of color that leaves them fighting against the controlling images for their group. These controlling images vary in negativity depending on where one finds themselves on the racial hierarchy. While Blacks and some Latino/as are subject to images of laziness, incompetence, or anger, Asian people are viewed as model minorities. This image marks them as relatively hard-working and high-achieving.[6] The processes of commodification reduce all employees of color to controlling images, but because the content of these images differs by group, so do the effects.

Asian employees in my study recognized that stereotypes about their group were different than those about Black and Latino/a employees. One South Asian assistant professor recalled how he experienced racism growing up but felt that it was not as pronounced in the academic realm. "While I am a person of color and, I'm sure in my life I have experienced racism, I'm not quite as marginalized as Black or Brown people in America. Within the context of academic STEM, my race and skin color are generally viewed as a positive thing and a privilege and not the opposite." The general positivity about his race puts this professor in a position where he does not experience the same threats to personal legitimacy as his Black and Latino/a counterparts. The model minority myth is harmful in other ways, for example by adding pressure for Asian employees to meet excessively high expectations. Still, employees who I spoke with saw it mostly as a net positive. This is in line with other studies that have examined Asian American workplace experiences.[7]

Another aspect that varies along the lines of racial hierarchy is the degree of isolation. While I have shown how Black and Latino/a employees often lack the social support that might ameliorate job strain, that was not true to the same extent for Asian employees. Asian employees spoke of their frequent social interactions with white coworkers. "So, you know, we've had dinner at each other's houses. We've gone out for lunches and brunch on weekends." This higher level of acceptance is in line with the relative integration of Asians in other areas such as neighborhoods. The ability of Asian employees to reach into white networks within their workplaces creates greater opportunities for collaboration and the sharing of information.[8]

Being in white social circles can also give Asian employees a front row seat to anti-Black racism. An East Asian pastor in the Deep South encountered this as the only person of color at an otherwise all-white party. "I was invited to a party, and they start talking about Black people. And I'm just listening. So, one of the gentlemen uses the N word. And so that's when I just got furious, like, 'You coward! I bet you will not say that word in front of a Black person!'" After this outburst, the white friend who brought this pastor to the party explained that the racial slur should be forgiven because of the individual's upbringing. In this way, the pastor was let in on not only the racist outburst but also the rationales that allow such outbursts to continue in polite company. This incident did not make the pastor feel like he was safe from racism. On the contrary, he left thinking, "I wonder what you say about me behind my back?"

As this pastor rightly ascertained, honorary white is not the same as white. The fragility of this honorary status was all too evident with the violence perpetrated by persons of all races against Asian persons during the height of the COVID-19 pandemic.[9] A Chinese American engineer in the Midwest put it this way, "No matter how hard I work or how achieved I am, I will always not be white."

Not being white comes with an uncertain status. Instead of being unambiguously accepted, Asian employees were relatively accepted if they would assent to the racial order and strive to be as close to white as possible—by not speaking out against racist comments, for example. This limited level of agency creates a conflict for Asian employees between the path to assimilation and the one of solidarity with their Black and Brown colleagues. One assistant professor who reflected on her choice put it this way:

> Being a Chinese American person has always made me feel like I'm in this kind of nebulous in-between where it's like, well, I'm not white, but like, I'm also a person of color who's not necessarily marginalized in the same way that like my Black and Brown colleagues are. And so what? What does that mean for me? And I think that sometimes the narrative turns into, well then, do what you need to do to assimilate with the people in power, who are the

white people. And I don't feel like that's the way I want to do things.

Instead of assimilating, this professor views her role as an ally of sorts. Not someone who is subject to the same inequities but is tasked to fight them.

One Black West Coast pastor also noted the choice for Asian employees between solidarity and assimilation. He compared himself to his Asian American coworker: "I think it's part of the Asian dynamic where he would be fine to stay under the radar. Some [Asians] will say that they've chosen to not engage the conversation for fear of rocking the boat, the whole model minority status." Here again, there is a choice between engaging issues of race and holding on to model minority status. Choosing not to engage seems to be a criterion for retaining honorary white status.

Asian employees who fought against the racial structure by rejecting assimilation toward whiteness faced both some ridicule from inside their communities as well as some of the additional burdens experienced by their Black and Brown colleagues. Sarah Hak is an assistant professor who developed a strong race consciousness during her childhood, as her family owned a store in a majority Black neighborhood. This contributed to her high identification as a person of color. Other Asian people were sometimes confused when she identified in this way. "When I talk to Asian people, and I'm like, 'Oh, yeah, I'm a woman of color.' They're like, 'Really? You identify as a woman of color?' I was like, 'Well, do you think I'm white?' And they're like, 'Well, no, but . . .'" The liminal space that Asian people sometimes find themselves in racially left this a conversation without a conclusion.

When Asian employees identify with other people of color, they become increasingly subject to the minority tax. Hak reported seeing her race increasingly used as a resource in diversity efforts once she signaled her willingness to engage.

Now that it's known on campus that I engage pretty deeply about diversity work, I think that my race has been used as a resource. I'm sure that there's plenty of Asian Americans in STEM that don't engage and that do see themselves as part of the white contingent of faculty. So, I'm not sure that they were necessarily expecting that initially from me. Now when there's some diversity thing that needs to be done, people come to me. It's almost like once you engage in this community, there is a service burden and tax associated with it.

Hak's account of being able to avoid diversity work until she indicated her desire to engage mirrors the account of another Asian American assistant professor. When I asked him about his diversity work for the university, he replied, "I haven't put myself out in a position to; I haven't volunteered myself for such a position." As I illustrate in the next two sections, Black and Latino/a employees do not have to volunteer to be implicated in diversity efforts.

Asian employees experienced what I call *conditional commodification*. Their position as representatives of diversity seemed conditioned upon their acceptance or rejection of the broader racial order. Those who accepted honorary white status, distancing themselves from other employees of color, were rewarded with lower expectations around diversity activities that created a heavier workload for other employees of color. They were evaluated in many ways "just like a white counterpart." Asian employees who chose to fight against white supremacy, however, found themselves subject to diversity ideology's heavy workload.

Representatives of Diversity: Black Employee Experiences

Hak recognized the conditional commodification she experienced once she chose to stand in solidarity with other people of color, but she also reflected on the heavier responsibilities she saw Black faculty members saddled with. While she did not pay the minority tax until she signaled her willingness to, the minority tax is not optional for Black faculty because of their position in the racial hierarchy. When asked how her race was used as a resource for her university, she mentioned that it was not used at first, compared to the Black faculty she worked with. "I don't think that they've necessarily used my ethnic background as a resource. I definitely do think that they have done it for others, especially Black faculty. I think that they get used as resources quite a bit."

Sociologists have speculated that diversity policies are particularly anti-Black because of the spotlight they shine on Black people as signals of an appropriately multicultural environment.[10] The employees I spoke with confirm this assertion. Black employees disproportionately bear the weight of being seen as the representatives of diversity and necessary to diversity conversations. This burden expresses itself in heightened service commitments, even as compared to other employees of color; responsibility for mentorship of other employees of color; and the obligation to correct incidents of racism via their own labor. If diversity is a commodity, Black employees are the most eagerly traded.

What is interesting about the high level of commodification that Black employees experience is that other employees of color recognize it. Asian and Latino / a employees mentioned, often with gratitude, the disproportionate work taken on by Black employees. One West Coast Latino was lamenting the additional service demands he faced until he reflected on the burdens placed on a Black faculty member in his department: "You know, honestly, I think she might have even higher demands than I do. Looking back into it, it's just we have very few female African American professors, and I think in terms of demand, my impression at least, that she might have even higher demands than I do." Another, when asked whether Black employees are asked to do more service, said, "They are in all those committees. They always are, if there is an equity task force or equity committee. All of them are."

Black employees agree with this assessment. As one Black professor compared his treatment to a Latina colleague, he commented, "People kinda treated her differently [than me]; when they spoke about diversity, they always spoke in Black/white terms." Another Black professor on the East Coast, reflecting on the level to which his time and attention were sought when compared to an Asian professor of the same rank, said, "They had an investment in being seen as pro-Black that I have not seen any evidence of being interested in being seen as pro-Asian. I don't see any evidence of people feeling the need to fight over his corpse the way that they felt the need to fight over mine. Obviously, because Blackness just signifies something different than Asianness does."

The legitimacy Black employees provide to workplaces is especially important in response to charges of racism. After an incident at one university that involved reckoning with past racism, the first response was to hire several Black faculty members. As one professor involved told me, "So, it seems like this diversity effort is centered around Black faculty. And I think that has to do with the Confederate flag thing. All of that backlash from last year; there were people in the yearbooks from the eighties in blackface with the Confederate flag. I could be wrong, but just from what I see is, it seems like it's focused on Black faculty." Diversity is valuable in part because it insulates organizations from charges of racism; based on these examples, Black employees provide better insulation than other racial groups.

The long-standing association between diversity and Black employees has afforded Black individuals predominance in diversity offices and multiculturalism centers compared to other racial groups. This longevity has built a specific sort of cultural capital that Black employees have passed along to others, specifically Latino/as. One Latino professor located in the Midwest noted the strength that Latino faculty gain from the presence, support, and experience of Black faculty. In this case, the two groups shared one faculty association. "We've [Latino faculty] learned a lot from them. And they've been very generous teaching us, coaching us about what works, doesn't work, who we need to talk to. We do notice that they have more clout, historically."

While Black employees provide this mentorship willingly, their disproportionate role in supporting other employees of color adds to their already heightened workloads as representatives of diversity. This uncompensated work shows up even at more informal work events. One Latina talked about the attentiveness a Black faculty member showed in ensuring she did not make missteps while socializing early in her career.

A lot of the mentoring that I have gotten has been from Black faculty, especially the chair of the Black Studies. I don't know why he does this. When I started, I would be at the college chatting with random people. I would start to say whatever was on my mind, and then he would come and get me. And he'd be like, "Oh, excuse me. I have to steal her away." He's like, "Why are you talking about that with that person?" At first, I was like, "Who does he think he is to tell me who I can and can't talk to?" Now, I think I understand a little bit better because I've asked him. He's like, "You were promising things to the dean with a glass of wine in your hand. Why? Don't do that. You were telling the dean that you had an idea. You don't have ideas; you don't have tenure."

This Black faculty member has the experience to know that ideas mean work for professors of color, work that untenured professors cannot afford to do if they intend to meet their other commitments. He steps in for a professor outside of his department to make sure she has the best chance to succeed.

Latino / a and Asian employees also perceive that Black employees are on the receiving end of the majority of the racial incidents. One Latino professor initially thought his treatment was roughly equivalent to that of the Black professors on campus. He looked at their relative experiences differently after there was a document circulated protesting racist incidents experienced by Black faculty members. He reasoned, "I think differently after these professors shared the things that they shared. Those incidents are specific racist acts against Black faculty. I think it is different. Completely different. I'm sure they had to go through a lot of things that I don't even want to imagine."

Racial incidents happen in workplaces that do not subscribe to diversity ideology, but in diverse organizations, acute experiences of racism combine with heavier service burdens because Black employees, as representatives of diversity, are expected to fix the racism that they face. For example, an Asian corporate employee in the South discussed her Black coworker's training of the staff. "One of my coworkers had to teach our other coworkers about microaggressions. And we were talking about hair, and there was someone she corrected, 'You do not touch my hair.' I was just sitting there and my jaw like fell over. Like, when is that ever appropriate? I just think it's exhausting." This Black employee's job is not diversity training, it is recruiting. Yet, she is subject to having her hair inappropriately touched and then has to turn around and train her coworkers on microaggressions. This is a double burden that deepens the effects of commodification.

In addition to being the representatives of diversity, Black employees have to contend with controlling images of themselves that are overwhelmingly negative. These negative stereotypes—as to their competence, worth, and intelligence—create environments where Black employees brought in under diversity initiatives are subject to micromanagement. Craig Henderson, a Black associate pastor on the West Coast, describes feeling constrained in his job. The constant questioning he received from his supervisors also led him in turn to question himself and his own competence. He recalled, "It was questions as far as, man, you sure you wanna do this? You know? And so, I was doubting. I'm crossing my t's and dotting my i's. I was being doubted more than just making sure that I had all my ducks in a row." He contrasted this with what he saw for his coworkers. "I just think they [white pastors], you know, they were taken more seriously. They felt the freedom; they had so much more freedom to be creative and fail."

Finally, Black employees' social interactions with white coworkers tend to be fraught. As mentioned in the previous discussion on social support, Black employees found fewer opportunities to build relationships that were personally fulfilling or that helped with getting the work done. Henderson also had a hard time connecting with his coworkers, particularly on mandatory retreats that he attended with the staff. These retreats were intensely focused on physical activities that this pastor did not enjoy. "I can tell you so much about pastors' retreats, and how we are playing spikeball. You think any Black folks are playing spikeball?" This pastor recognized that his belonging was sacrificed for that of his white coworkers' belonging. As he poignantly judged, "I couldn't fully be myself because the reality is they are [being themselves]."

Based on the perspective of the Black employees and their coworkers, this group paid the highest price related to diversity. As representatives of diversity, Black employees experienced disproportionately heavy workloads due to their prevalence on task forces and committees, provided mentorship to other groups in their workplaces, and bore the brunt of racial incidents as well as the responsibility for protesting or educating after such incidents. Black employees also found themselves battling against more negative controlling images and experienced less social support from white coworkers when compared to Asian employees.

Not Quite Honorary White: Latino/a Experiences

Latino/as who have lighter skin are frequently considered to be in the category of honorary white. Among the Latino/as I spoke with, many experienced this color privilege and brought it up during interviews. One professor at a Midwestern liberal arts college commented how not only he but also his students noticed privilege based on skin color in academia.

> A few years ago, when I was a teaching assistant, a student asked me why all the Latinos in our grad program were white. And he said that there were no darker-skinned or Indigenous looking people in our program among the faculty even. And ever since he said that, I've always had that in the back of my mind. Even though we're Latinos in academia, we're really light-skinned. We're still light-skinned. There's not a lot of Afro Latinos; there's not a lot of Indigenous heritage. So, I would say that that most of us are Whitetinos.

Being a "Whitetino," or a white person of Latino/a ethnicity, leaves lighter-skinned Latino/as in a liminal space. Another professor who, along with his wife, experienced color privilege said, "And so you don't necessarily feel accepted in the average Latino social space. But then also, you also don't fit in the world of whiteness. And we're in this, it's very much a space of flux. I guess that it's kind of a source of frustration all the time." A Mexican American pastor on the West Coast echoed this in-betweenness: "Sometimes subconsciously, we play up our whiteness for the sake of fitting in, and sometimes we play up our Latinoness in order to fit in; we've had to become adaptable in order to thrive." This back-and-forth left the pastor feeling "ni de aquí, ni de allá." He was left neither here nor there in terms of his racial identity and the group he could comfortably fit into.

The space of flux in which Latino/a employees found themselves was not equivalent to the Asian experience of being honorary white. Latino/as' marginalization and status as people of color were unquestioned, as was their responsibility to participate in diversity initiatives. As one Latino professor put it, "If we talk about the Black tax or minority tax, to go out and represent the institution, to go out and support other students of color, to me, it's a burden that falls upon many of us to go above and beyond." In this way, their experiences were similar to, but not the same as, those of Black employees.

Sociologist Nilda Florez-Gonzalez, in her book on the experiences of Latino/a millennials, describes the ways that Latino/as find themselves in a racial middle.[11] Unlike Bonilla-Silva's one-tier "honorary white," Flores's millennials see multiple steps between Black and white that are occupied in different ways by Asian, Latino/a, and Indigenous people. Similar to those in my research, Latino/as in her study saw their position as below that of Asians but above that of Blacks in the racial hierarchy. She asserts they end up lower than Asian Americans because Latino/as' foreignness comes with a stigma of illegality. They end up higher than African Americans, but partially share the stigma associated with native minorities as "underachievers."

The employees I spoke with most often wrestle with the charge of being labeled as underachievers due to the stigma of being associated with diversity initiatives. As discussed in chapter 2, Latino/a employees often had to counter people who referred to them as diversity hires. As Asian employees experience controlling images about their group projecting ideas of hypercompetence onto them, so Latino/a employees experience the specter of incompetence. A Latino professor at a liberal arts college, when asked if he struggles with his identity at work, replied, "I guess I struggle and I worry about my colleagues. I want them to know that I'm more than just a diversity quota." For Latino/a employees, making a mistake poses more than a temporary setback. It may mean confirming their colleagues' worst stereotypes about them. The added pressure of controlling images about Latino/as, as opposed to Asians, creates a marked difference in experiences.

Another way in which the position of Latino/as seems to differ from that of Asian Americans in the workplace is in terms of social distance from whites. Asian Americans can access white social networks in order to gain valued resources. Latino/as, however, report feeling more distant from whites and Asians and closer in social distance to Blacks, given their common marginalization.[12] One Latina assistant professor spoke about how this social distance made her distrust her white coworkers.

> I work well with everybody. I think closer with the faculty of color. I don't, as I said to this Black professor, I don't trust white women. I think they are unreliable. But they are my colleagues. So, I work with them, and I keep my door shut. My students know that my door is closed, but I'm there, so they already know how to reach me. These women, we are not friends; we are colleagues. I'm not going to tell you my life. Like, this is the work that we need to do, and that's it.

This professor went on to explain how she overheard her white women colleagues giving each other different advice privately than they gave to a colleague of color publicly. "I see them saying one thing in the meeting and then saying a different thing in the hallway." The distrust generated by this event perpetuated the distance between this professor and her coworkers.[13]

The experiences of Latino/as that point to a distinct racial middle are in line with reports from other studies.[14] Interestingly, although management positions host a group of lighter-skinned and highly educated Latino/as, employees still do not have the privileges of honorary whites. Instead, Latino/as experience threats to legitimacy and subjugated identity because of controlling images that challenge rather than boost their competence alongside lack of social support.

The Anti-Blackness of Diversity

Because Blackness is more associated with diversity than other racial groups, Black employees bore the heaviest burdens of commodification. For example, not one Asian person in my sample traced their hiring back to a racial incident, whereas at least one Latino and multiple Black employees did. Be it within academia or church, in the aftermath of racial incidents, bringing in a Black employee carried the cachet of antiracism, and along with that the need for new Black employees to be shown off in diversity displays. Hiring Black employees did more to insulate organizations against claims of racism than either Latino/a or Asian employees; this insulation is a key benefit to signaling diversity.

Like many other inequalities related to race, these results show the costs of diversity to be particularly anti-Black. Still, commodification is far from displaying a Black/non-Black binary.[15] Instead, each group experiences their own costs as they negotiate the effects of diversity ideology in their organizations. Latino/a and Asian employees find themselves in distinct positions relative to the effects of diversity ideology. Latino/as are not quite honorary white, and Asians only honorary white if they agree to assimilate. These positions show the precarity of status in the racial hierarchy for all assigned to any group except white. The racial structure in which all three groups are embedded constrains their options and experiences in diverse organizations.

5 "*I'm Improving It for Us*"

Diversity Ideology for Employees of Color

This place was fucked up when you got here; it will be fucked up when you leave here. All you can control is how much you let it fuck you up in the process.

TRESSIE MCMILLAN COTTOM, author, sociologist, and MacArthur Fellow

Tea Lacaba is a slight, twenty-something, Puerto Rican woman who can aptly be described as a bundle of energy. Her quick, clipped sentences have marketing knowledge woven in like an intricate tapestry. When she speaks about her experiences working for a midsized coffee company, however, Lacaba's energy dips and she blinks back tears as she describes how she felt used by her company. During her tenure there, she would occasionally be invited on business trips and given no clear task. These trips not only took time away from her normal work responsibilities, they also caused her enormous anxiety. "I just recall being on a trip, and I keep on asking what to do or how I can help . . . and there's nothing, but they're paying me, so." Far from being happy to receive a paycheck for simply showing her face, Lacaba questioned her job performance and utility to the company: "I was extremely paranoid. I think

I recall two trips where I was frantically asking for something to do." Eventually, her manager's comments allowed Lacaba to infer that she was brought along so her employers wouldn't show up with an all-white team. A clear case of commodification.

Despite her disaffection for her company's actions, Lacaba did not draw back from her responsibilities. She didn't put her head down and do the bare minimum. Instead, she did more work than she was hired or paid for. In addition to being brought along on these trips to display diversity, Lacaba supported the company's diversity by making exceptional efforts to get to know other employees of color and advocate for them on labor issues. Although she worked in the front office, where she was the only person of color, Lacaba spent significant portions of her day interacting with the majority Black manufacturing workers, a task well outside her role in marketing. "A lot of people in the front office didn't take time to get to know their other coworkers in the manufacturing side of the plant. I was volunteering. I was spending thirty minutes to an hour a day just talking to people." When Lacaba's time was already being misused to visibly display diversity, why would she give her company even more time by supporting the employees of color that her company refused to?

To answer this question, we must shift our focus to the commonsense views and logics employees of color apply concerning diversity: *their* diversity ideology. How does Lacaba, knowing that her company is using her for diversity purposes, conceptualize her role in the workplace and chart a course of action?

In the previous three chapters, I have discussed the effects of commodification, which is a tenet of the dominant diversity ideology.[1] But this formulation of diversity ideology focuses on white people and institutions to the exclusion of people of color.[2] Here I turn instead to the diversity ideologies reflected by employees of color in their lives and work. First, I will elucidate how the diversity ideology of employees of color may diverge from the dominant diversity ideology. Then, in the balance of the chapter, I will draw out the tenets of diversity ideology for employees of color and how this ideology affects their actions in the workplace.

Ideologies of diversity found in white institutions are hegemonic or taken for granted in society. Given the pervasiveness of these ideologies, employees of color are left with two choices: ascertain the dominant ideologies and act instrumentally within them, or formulate their own systems of meaning around diversity in the face of them.

If an employee of color were to take an instrumental approach, they might utilize the workplace's need for diversity to their best advantage. As discussed in chapter 2, diversity ideology rests on a neoliberal market mentality that turns people's attributes into marketable possessions. Aligning with this view and acting instrumentally would mean deriving economic value from one's racial identity. Sociologist Michel Foucault looked at this as becoming an entrepreneur of oneself.[3] That is, one who rationally determines the best return on one's own human capital and pursues it accordingly. Employees of color could extend this idea to their racial capital, actively accepting commodification where it leads to personal gain.

A rejection of economic self-maximization may conversely indicate an independent diversity ideology for employees of color. By refusing to think of their racial identity and time as simply a commodity for others, they undercut the neoliberal foundations on which diversity rests. Rejecting a solely economic calculus allows employees of color to make sense of diversity in their own way, thereby refusing to normalize whites' moral preferences of individual attainment.[4]

As it turns out, there is evidence of both an instrumental and an independent approach to diversity ideology; these contradictory impulses coexist. Employees of color create their own shared meanings around diversity, rejecting self-maximization in order to assist others. They also react instrumentally in the face of dominant diversity ideologies, leveraging their racial identity for gain where possible. Note that neither of these is a preferred choice. Each represents what is possible given the societal landscape of race, diversity, and organizational prerogatives.

When employees of color undertake their own diversity ideology, they reflect *diversity as philanthropy*. Diversity as philanthropy is exemplified by Tea Lacaba's explanations for her actions to voluntarily spend time with the manufacturing workers. She indicated that her racial identity would not allow her to make a different choice: "When it comes to taking a stance or taking a team, I'm gonna have to do it. It was just very clear to me that my whole life that like, I would rather be with the people who work their butt off. I'm doing what I can." In her statement, Lacaba identifies herself with the Black manufacturing team above her white, front office peers. She also shares that this identification is a lifelong orientation. She knows which team she wants to be on and will always do what she can, even if it costs her in other ways. Orientations like Lacaba's emerge when an organization's desire to be seen as diverse meets a culture of collective uplift, where members of a group feel responsible for the success of other members of that group (however defined). Employees conceptualizing diversity as philanthropy, then, often endanger their own advancement, giving time and energy to aid others.

At the same time, employees of color have no choice but to respond to the diversity ideology of white people and institutions given its pervasiveness. *Diversity as opportunity* and *diversity as resource* are both instrumental responses to dominant diversity ideology, wherein employees focus on their own gain. Employees who treat *diversity as opportunity* understand what their employers expect from them as employees of color and see their commodification as part of the bargain. Because Black and Latino/a applicants are less likely to be hired than similarly qualified white applicants, they are fine with being hired for diversity reasons, seeing that it might be the only reason these organizations would hire them at all.[5] If diversity is the reason for their hiring, they conclude it is best to be thankful and make the most of the opportunity. These employees decide, no matter the reason for their hiring, they can use it as an opening to show what they can really do.

Other employees come to see *diversity as resource.* These employees leverage a shift in the balance of power from their employers to themselves. This shift often happens when their organization's legitimacy as diverse comes under scrutiny; as a result, their employers' need for them increases. Recognizing their power, the employees of color perceive that they deserve a more equitable share of the gains from their commodification. Employees who use diversity as resource reject subjugated identity and deflect some of the work demands of commodification.

Diversity as philanthropy, diversity as opportunity, and diversity as resource are three tenets of the diversity ideology held by employees of color. These tenets are not mutually exclusive and coexist in everyday action. A professor may see diversity as resource, for example, but turn around and spend some of their additional power helping students of color succeed.

Diversity as Philanthropy

Racial Outsourcing and Equity Labor

Like Tea Lacaba, employees of color take on additional tasks to combat organizational inequities all the time. Termed racialized equity labor by sociologists Laura Hamilton, Kelly Nielsen, and Veronica Lerma in their study of universities, these tasks include any "intentional efforts to support marginalized communities and challenge inequitable organizational structures."[6] Different from diversity displays, this labor is not about painting a superficial veneer of diversity but is actually designed to serve constituencies of color. Unfortunately, this work is done in addition to already heavy work requirements, costing employees of color in terms of time, well-being, and opportunities for advancement.

Equity labor is prompted by the gaps that organizations leave as they strive for diversity. In her book *Flatlining,* sociologist Adia Harvey Wingfield called these organizational shortfalls racial outsourcing. Workplaces that promote themselves as diverse, but do little to support constituencies of color, outsource the work of equity to employees of color through their omission. Wingfield catalogs the ways that Black doctors, nurses, and medical technicians all go above and beyond to mentor Black medical students, advocate for the fair treatment of Black patients, and help Black patients navigate the complexities of the medical system, respectively. Wingfield finds: "They do this by dedicating themselves to communities of color even to their own financial detriment, and by committing themselves to creating opportunities for other workers of color in the absence of institutional support."[7] Although Wingfield studies this phenomenon among Black employees,

Latino/a and Asian American employees also engage in racial equity labor.

Despite the attention to what employees of color do, there is relatively less scholarship on *why* they do what they do. It has been taken for granted by organizations and many scholars that employees of color will engage in this giving behavior without sufficiently interrogating how this behavior is prompted. The reason why is what I turn to next.

Socialized to Say Yes

The National Center for Faculty Development and Diversity includes within its core curriculum "The Art of Saying No." Just as we have learned from the War on Drugs, telling people to just say no is of limited effectiveness. Professors who are underrepresented minorities still spend twice as much time in mentoring as white faculty.[8] While mentoring is critical to student successes, it can be detrimental to professors'. Many colleges and universities heavily weight research productivity in performance reviews, significantly disadvantaging those who mentor students at the expense of their own research productivity.

Educators Emily L. Moore and J. Herman Blake use the concept "inherent philanthropy" to describe how Black faculty spend their time.[9] The philanthropy of these faculty is not located in the paid work of academia but in additional uncompensated and underrecognized service work, like student mentorship and committee assignments. Examining their own work priorities, Moore and Blake describe how their socialization made certain service work inescapable. They were tasked to leave their university community better than they found it; this philanthropic drive led them to take on study groups, mentorship, and advocacy for students beyond what was expected and generally accomplished by other professors. Failing to do so would mean letting down parents, grandparents, mentors, and a host of ancestors who expected and taught this very behavior over generations.

The socialization Moore and Blake talk about can be thought of as a form of cultural capital, or dispositions that are passed on starting in childhood and become second nature.[10] Moore and Blake's upbringing socialized them to value service to others in a way that found ready avenues in the context of a university not designed to well serve students of color. Because this idea of serving others was deeply ingrained, just saying no would fight against everything they were taught to be true. Cultural capital is often used to pass on generational advantages.[11] In the right structure, cultural capital emphasizing service to others would indeed be extremely valuable as people instinctively helped each other to succeed. The individualism and individual achievement that dominate most US-based organizations, however, means that the exercise of this cultural capital is economically detrimental to employees socialized to sacrifice individual achievement for collective uplift. Moore and Blake understood this calculus and what serving may cost them in individual achievement but did it anyway. This knowing sacrifice elevates the work of these employees to the level of philanthropy.

It feels jarring to define this work as philanthropy because it does not line up with what the public imagination applies to charitable giving. This is not the stuff of fundraising galas but rather a daily disposition toward others. Everyday types of giving may be severely underreported as givers do not necessarily think of what they do as philanthropy. But what Moore and Blake describe fits very well the accepted definition of philanthropy put forth by scholar Nancy Goldfarb. She calls philanthropy private giving for the public good or to ameliorate a social problem, recognizing "giving" as going beyond money to include "voluntary action, voluntary giving, and voluntary association."[12] Because it is so underreported, light needs to be shone on what constitutes this type of philanthropy and how it affects organizational dynamics.

Moore and Blake focus on the inherent philanthropy of Black faculty members; however, I find similar sacrificial work and rationales for that function across racial groups and organization types. This makes sense given the evidence for a culture of collective uplift across groups. For example, Latino / a corporate employees reject individualistic notions of achievement and Latino / a faculty members say they work to give back because true success is collective.[13] Asian American pastors advise each other and work collectively to gain acceptance in diverse churches.[14] When subject to diversity imperatives, I find that pastors create spaces for congregants of color; professionals mentor the minoritized employees around them; and professors create initiatives to benefit students of color. The widespread nature of this sacrificial work is remarkable given the differential racialization of each group and points to shared conceptions around what it means to be the object of diversity.

Religious Involvement

When employees of color explain the racial equity labor they do, they use rationales associated with philanthropy. One of the most reliable predictors of philanthropy is religious involvement.

Attendance at services, religious beliefs, and socialization have all been shown to increase levels of both religious and secular philanthropy.[15]

Employees' use of religious rationale to justify philanthropic activity was marked by appeals to an external, existential authority. Not surprisingly, I often heard this from pastors who asserted that their faith compelled them to remain in diverse churches, even when they recognized that these organizations were harmful for them. One Asian American pastor living in the Pacific Northwest worked for a church that prominently described its commitment to being "multiethnic" on its website. The church, itself, however, did very little to sustain this commitment. This pastor, who was hired to be an associate pastor for the church, created a fellowship group where congregants of color would gather and worship together. He did this on his own and of his own volition. As he told me: "For nine years, I grew, with no resources, a multiethnic, multigenerational community of about three hundred people." Within the church's overall membership of 1,800 members, this community was a space where congregants of color felt at home, sustaining the church's claims to diversity. It was also a place where women and people of color were in the preaching rotation and were given voice—an opportunity not afforded by the larger church. Although the fellowship was fruitful for its members, the additional work this pastor undertook cost him.

> It was more so leveraging my role to create space for others [but] I don't think I realized the toll. So fast forward seven years, you're talking to someone who's really tired, and there's been a lot of bruises and good intentions and results that ended up fracturing and trying to navigate. I think when you listen to the gospel

of Jesus right, you hear the message. And you see our Lord and Savior willing to sacrifice at every level. Right? It's the steps that He takes. He could have come as any kind of human, but He chooses to be born to poverty, right? He could have chosen to die in any kind of way. But He chooses to die in the most humiliating, right? So, at every level he chooses. And so, you hear this message of sacrifice.

For this pastor, following the example of Jesus means sacrificing for others, no matter the toll. He uses that sacrifice to make room for people of color to lead within the church by hiring within his sphere of influence and developing volunteer leaders.

Pastors, however, were not the only ones who gave religious rationale for their work within diverse organizations. Assistant professor Sam Johnson expressed a similar sentiment from his university in the Northeast. He credited his faith for energizing his responsiveness to students. Professor Johnson is the only Black tenure-track professor in his department, not an uncommon occurrence. This opens him up to experience commodification, such as being asked to represent the department at various events: "So, we have the candidates' day or when we have to meet people, the fact I'm Black, young and personable, they really want me. And they've asked me to come and appear at those things, right, where any white faculty is, you know, like, we'll take whoever we can get. But we really need you." These events, while minor in isolation, take time out of an already stretched schedule with publication and teaching expectations for tenure. He feels the weight of this additional work: "It is definitely an injustice in the sense that I feel like I have to do two jobs to get one paycheck. And my white colleagues get one paycheck to do one job."

Despite acknowledging the additional labor he is asked to do, Professor Johnson takes even more responsibility on himself, investing in students of color and creating space for them. When asked how he focuses this extra effort, he explained, "I believe that white students will have faculty who will look out for their best interests. I don't believe that Black students will have that. All my courses, they've all been majority students of color. That's because students of color know I'm here to serve them. Even as I know that the university is not set up for them." In this statement, Professor Johnson acknowledged that he works at a place not set up for students of color to thrive, and that he does work specifically to fill that gap. In his free hours, therefore, Professor Johnson takes the time to make sure these students do not fall through the cracks that are left for them. For him, this is what it means to value Black people for themselves: "To value Black people as people rather than valuing Black people as a moral lesson, a moral test, or some other form of relational entity to white people."

When asked to explain why he takes on this additional work and is willing to bear the burden in terms of time and energy, Professor Johnson turned to religious rationale:

> I mislearned many of the lessons of Black Pentecostalism such that I had a strong martyr complex the entire time. Like the entire goal of my life, if you asked me what it is that you're trying to do with your life, I would have said, I am trying to give my life away. The idea is to serve until you die. That's the request of Christ. And so, the notion of unfair suffering in exchange for mentoring Black students and seeing them grow. It just felt like that was my whole purpose in life. It didn't feel like an injustice to me so much as a fulfillment of what I was trying to do.

Johnson's upbringing as a Christian planted the seeds that caused him to endure his environment and how he was treated if he could provide guidance to the next generation. While this sacrifice could have been focused anywhere, collective uplift dictated that it find its expression in support of Black students. As a Black professor in a diverse university, suffering for the sake of Christ became part of his job description. In Johnson's case, diversity as philanthropy dictated that he spend nearly all of his time on campus; the walls of his apartment were empty after over a year in his role.

Experience

Another driver of philanthropy is knowledge about the need. People who have personal experience with a given need are more likely to have an awareness that leads to giving.[16]

Ayodele Marshall, our wealth manager from chapter 2, experiences commodification by being paraded in front of Black clients. His primary role also involves meeting mainly with clients of color. Outside of this, however, Marshall takes on his own form of outreach by taking on clients that others in his organization would reject out of hand. "[My counterparts] have a $250,000 or $500,000 minimum. I never turned anyone away. If you need help and you want help, I'll help you. I don't get paid for less than a specific amount, I feel like if somebody really wants help, I can spare forty-five minutes or an hour of my day to help someone."

Marshall's employer is not willing to pay him for the time he spends with low-net-worth clients. Yes, he still maintains a policy of seeing anyone who needs help. The probability of encountering such clients is enhanced by the fact that Marshall is assigned to primarily minority clients who, by virtue of the racial wealth gap, tend to have smaller accounts than the clients of Marshall's white coworkers.

When asked whether his policy of seeing anyone who wants help makes advancement within the company more difficult, Marshall admits that it does. Still, he is unwilling to compromise in this area despite the costs. "I'd have a hard time turning someone away who actually needs help, because I remember that was me. So, it's my competing priorities. It's my challenge, and just I'm still trying to figure it out. And how to accomplish both, you know?"

Marshall's rationale for spending time with these clients comes from his personal experience. His own story of being ignored in a financial institution creates an awareness of the problem minoritized persons face that drives his philanthropic view of time and energy.

> Part of the reason why I came into this field was because of my first experience. When I was a sophomore in college, I managed to save up a thousand dollars and I had heard about investing and saving. So, I take that thousand dollars, go to a bank and ask if I can meet with an advisor there. This guy did not want to give me the time of day at all. He ended up taking my money, opening up some stupid accounts, had me thinking that it's going to do something, you know, didn't have a plan for me, didn't really listen to me. It was literally a fifteen-minute meeting. I'm thinking, 'Hey, I'm doing something, something's happening.' I checked three years later; I made eleven cents. Nothing happened. And it pushed me to jump into this industry to make those changes, to really step in and create more opportunities.

The sting of being ignored by a wealth manager remains in the forefront for Marshall as he decides that no one who comes to him will have that same experience. Marshall is ambitious and wants to advance to the position of a key decision maker within his company so that he can be even more helpful to others currently ignored in his industry. Ironically, Marshall's racial equity labor may make that aspiration much more difficult. Still, taking a different tact seems unfathomable to Marshall. "But I can't stop. I can't," he affirmed. Marshall is committed to maintaining the current trajectory of giving his time and hoping that he can do so while still achieving his career goals. On an apples-to-apples basis, it is hard to imagine how he posts the numbers to earn promotion above coworkers who are not following this strategy. Wealth managers are evaluated on the size and performance of their portfolio of accounts. If Marshall's white counterparts are earning across all of their accounts and Marshall is only earning on a subset of his smaller accounts, Marshall will have to make herculean efforts to catch up. The way that his job is structured penalizes, rather than rewards, treating all people as equally important.

Altruism

Altruism is another driver of philanthropy.[17] Altruism can be defined as "behavior intended to benefit another, even when doing so may risk or entail some sacrifice to the welfare of the actor."[18] When driven by altruism, employees of color give even when they recognize they may be harming themselves or their own career. This drive is pronounced with professors in the sample. Martin Estime is an assistant professor at a Midwestern research university. He has misgivings about the amount of service work he takes on, knowing he is not necessarily doing the best thing for his career. Despite this, he does not feel as though he could make another choice. "But here's where I'm not sure if I'm falling into the trap of the minority, right, I feel like it's part of what I'm here to do. So, I have a personal commitment to it, and I wouldn't not do it. I feel that it's necessary. And if I don't do it, maybe it's not going to get done." Estime's language here is telling: the idea of service work being a "trap" that is specifically laid for minorities. He knows that it can take time that could be spent on research work that would be more helpful to his career advancement. But although service work focused on students is not the part of his job Estime is primarily evaluated on, he believes service work is what he is there for. He also believes that no one else will step in if he doesn't step up.

Mentors often encourage faculty of color to avoid excess service and make time decisions benefiting their long-term careers. What this advice prompting faculty to say no misses, however, is that faculty do not want to. With a framework of diversity as philanthropy, working for minoritized students is the only choice that makes sense. Employees of color are fully cognizant of the choices they are making and the disadvantages that these choices engender. With that knowledge, they do it anyway, investing more time in their students than is wise for career advancement.

I asked Estime what disadvantages or additional work he as a Latino professor takes on so that his university can appear diverse. "I mean, it definitely takes more work. I could be fulfilling all my duties under my contract and expectations of a tenure-track faculty without doing any of that [diversity] work." Yet, Estime doesn't continue doing work to support students of color out of ignorance. He knows the trade-off between student support and research productivity and chooses the students anyway. "If I publish one less paper, but I can do this, and I'm still doing enough in the research part, then I'll write one less paper."

Even in places where he could legitimately say no, Estime chooses not to. He places fulfillment at work and serving the students he focuses on above publishing more papers. This is not a small sacrifice. Other professors of color have paid the price for making this choice. One Black assistant professor I interviewed had an exceptional record of service to students and promoting student activism. Ultimately, he fell one paper short of receiving tenure at his Midwestern research university. When asked if he regrets his decision, he is adamant that he did the right thing:

> I believe in what I did and I see the benefit for the people I did it for. The flaw was not uplifting my students at the expense of publishing one more article. That one more out. You can only choose to win or lose at all times. I lost on my terms. I will always choose to lose on my terms. Put me in the same position again, I will choose to lose on my terms.

This assistant professor refused to see himself as powerless in the face of the university system, even if doing what he believed in meant "losing."

For employees of color, work is more than a simple economic exchange to be maximized. When making decisions that endanger their very livelihood, the primary goal is that others can be enriched. The phenomenon of altruism among employees of color is often taken for granted, but certainly should not be. Most people choose to do things at work that will advance them in that setting. These employees knowingly do exactly the opposite. When their altruism results in the expected disadvantages, even affecting the money they bring home to their families, employees of color reject the idea that their work for others was a mistake. They aver that they would do it again.

Collective Uplift

Finally, regardless of their rationale, collective (racial) uplift was front and center in the minds of employees in my sample. Racial uplift ideology was captured by sociologist W. E. B. Du Bois in his writings on the talented tenth.[19] It advocates that those with resources use them to help the disprivileged, and in so doing advance the race as a whole. This idea still has resonance today in work on Black philanthropy. When driven by collective uplift, givers focus on causes that protect Black racial identity from racist narratives.[20] Giving to Black causes also has benefits for the giver, allowing the nurture of Black identity for upper and middle classes and showing the centrality of race to their lives. (Middle- and upper-class Latino/as show similar patterns, giving to Latino/a-centric causes.[21]) Such giving also fills gaps left when whites do not give to racially focused causes.

Bossie Renner, an assistant professor in a Southern liberal arts university, exhibited collective uplift in her willingness to give up working at a place she would feel more comfortable to create an accommodating space for Black students on her campus. "I could go to a place that's, like, a minority-serving institution, Hispanic-serving institution, HBCU, right? I could definitely do that. And I think my work and my presence will be valuable. But I also feel like my presence is very valuable here for the Black students who don't see themselves represented anywhere." Renner has faced challenges in the university where she works, which hired a number of Black faculty after a nationally publicized incident of racism damaged the school's reputation. Still, she reasons that being there is important, not for the university's reputation, or even her own well-being, but for the sake of students who will be without representation if she is not there.

Renner's priority in being present for Black students shows in everything from her office décor to the classes she teaches. "I have a pan-African flag in my office, like here is Blackness. I have students coming in who are not even in my classes who just need to, want to, be in this space. Next semester, I'm teaching a class and I have sixteen students; thirteen of them are Black. Twelve of them are Black women. So, for them to be able to have that experience, that means a lot to me." Renner creates an environment where not only her own students but any Black student on campus can come and find an oasis from a generally unsupportive and sometimes openly hostile environment. She is able to do this by signaling her own position as a Black woman in her office décor and welcoming attitude toward students, in the end benefiting students who find a place of belonging.

Instead of being at a school where Blackness is centered, Renner chooses to work for a predominantly white organization and make the environment more welcoming for students who wouldn't otherwise see themselves represented. When asked why she is willing to sacrifice her own comfort for that opportunity, Renner speaks about the collective and what her presence means for the people who will come after her:

I think in general my ideas are much more collective ideas. Like how can I, even when I'm grinding for myself, improve the collective. How is this going to make it better for the next Black woman, next year? I don't think white people in general [think like this] and not in these professional settings. It's like, I need to publish my thing, I need to do this. It's not like I need to work with this Black student because she needs to get an opportunity so that she can go to grad school. I'm thinking all those things, right? I make the decisions that I make professionally and personally. I don't think across the board people are thinking about all that stuff when they're making decisions.

Renner cites considerations that she sees as different than those of her white coworkers. Because of the importance of collective uplift to Renner, success means helping other Black people succeed and providing opportunities that they wouldn't otherwise have.

An oft-repeated phrase that exemplifies collective uplift is the need to "pay it forward." Because these employees of color have themselves benefited from the investment of those who came before them, they value continuing in that pattern. A Latino professor at a Midwestern liberal arts college expressed this sentiment as he described the sort of mentorship he received. His desire was to ensure the next generation of students received the same. "I've definitely got to do right by them. I see myself in a lot of them. First-generation, low-income students that came from similar backgrounds in terms of home situation, having immigrant parents, speaking Spanish. Especially for my Latino students, I gotta be there for them to pay it forward." Strong identification with these students and his own history propel this professor to give to his students what he has received. Paying it forward comes from employees' gratitude of mentors or opportunities they had in the past.

They will do what it takes to make sure these advantages don't end with them.

Diversity as Opportunity

Diversity as philanthropy was not the only one way that employees of color thought about diversity and their place in it. Another is *diversity as opportunity*. Employees who see diversity as opportunity are pragmatic and act instrumentally in the face of their commodification. They understand that their racial capital is of special value to their employer and are willing to trade that value for jobs and visibility. One Latino professor reasoned, "I imagine my face is in a brochure somewhere as evidence of inclusion. But I don't think it's all that bad because it has created opportunity for people like me to be able to get a job." This does not mean there are not mixed feelings about this commodification. One Black corporate employee worried about being pigeonholed by her work to serve communities of color: "I don't necessarily like it because I think I can cross cultures and racial boundaries. But sometimes you use it to your advantage, you know, you get opportunities, because you can relate to a particular audience." In the end, she figures the opportunities she receives outweigh the costs, although this is not the situation she would have chosen.

August Calvo, a Latino assistant professor at a small Midwestern university, was hired in response to an incident of racism. A trustee of the university had asked publicly whether the university wanted qualified faculty or faculty of color. This false dichotomy created enough angst to spark student protests, a new focus on diversity, and a cluster hire of faculty of color. All these diversity displays were accomplished in lieu of disciplining or removing the trustee who could make the lives of these new faculty more difficult. Calvo was not made aware of this incident at the time of his hiring but found out after arriving on campus.

When I asked Calvo how he felt when he learned that racist comments prompted his hiring, he was surprisingly upbeat:

> I actually have lots of positive things about it. (A) I got a job. So, I'm like . . . thanks, lady. It was awful sh** you said, but now I'm here. And (B) I went on to work with and mentor students who were leaders of color on campus. I've written letters of recommendation for them, and I write powerful letters for them too, because I owe [my job] to their work. Because they protested and demonstrated, the university took action, and I'm here. To a certain extent, it's a happy story, at least for me. So, how did I feel about it? I felt fine. I got mine, and positive things have happened. In the grand scheme of things, things are getting better and moving in the right direction.

Calvo has no compunction about the circumstances surrounding his hiring, He sees the situation as one that ultimately worked out in his favor and the favor of the Black and Latino/a students who protested for diverse faculty. In like manner, he frames the times that his race has been used as a resource for the university as a benefit back to him: "I get more attention. I would say it's probably a benefit to me. I am a part of a research project that we used students in, and our story got covered by the alumni magazine. So, if I make the news or do something, you know, I get coverage." Calvo expects this coverage will help him with his tenure case in the future.

Calvo exemplifies the attitude of those who view diversity as opportunity. He is happy to provide what the university requests and sees his commodification to help the university get past a racial incident as simply part of the bargain. Calvo does not take offense at diversity displays, such as the media coverage he receives, because it results in a job for him and a better environment for his students.

Brian Clemmons is another employee who sees diversity as opportunity. I spoke to Clemmons at his Midwestern home, which is decorated with the spoils of middle-class Blackness—Black art, a closet full of suits, and swag from his alma mater everywhere. Clemmons grew up in a working-class home; from a young age, he made it his business to live a more prosperous life as an adult and help others do the same. He was hired as the second Black pastor and second pastor of color ever at his church. What was most novel is that Clemmons was not a pastor at all before he was hired. He instead worked as a research scientist for a Fortune 500 company. It was made abundantly clear that he was being asked to shift career paths so that the church could promote diversity. "There wasn't any question as to the reason why I was hired. It was for my Blackness, for lack of a better term. To bring my cultural identity and help to influence the direction of the church as it moved forward." Despite his dreams of financial security, Clemmons took a significant pay cut to make this career change.

Clemmons admitted feeling a bit "odd" about the circumstances of his hiring. After being hired for his racial identity, he wrestled with where his value as a person was located. He reasoned, "I would say that even at my old company, I wasn't more valuable as an African American than I was as a scientist." Now,

Clemmons felt he only brought value as a Black man. In the end, Clemmons was able to rationalize his position by speaking of the other skills he knew he could contribute to the church over time. His hiring opened up space for him to prove himself in other ways. "Obviously, after being on staff after a period of time, I did go to seminary to get my Bible degree, and my administrative gifts showed out. So, eventually, I did move into roles to utilize those gifts. But starting out, I could understand if there were some other people on staff who were like, 'Who is this guy? He's not a Bible scholar.'"

Although Clemmons eventually found his place, the process was not without consequences for his self-concept. He went from seeing being Black as just part of himself to being something valued by his employer. This is an example of subjugated identity. Clemmons was forced to make as primary the identity most valuable to the church he worked for. He reasoned, "There was no training involved with becoming Black; it was just who I am. So, before I had never had any special value in that. I put value in being a scientist because I trained and worked hard for that. But now I was feeling valuable for being Black." Clemmons had one idea of his self-concept based on an identity that he worked hard to obtain, that of research scientist. In the environment of a church striving to be diverse, however, he was asked to trade that identity for the identity of Black pastor. While Clemmons struggled with this in himself, he gave up his corporate job to endure questioning about his abilities as someone who has not been trained as a pastor but is now working in a church. Through this action, Clemmons loses control over his identity and his right to define himself in favor of what his employer requires. Diversity provided an opportunity here, but not one Clemmons ever wanted.

Diversity as Resource

Other employees take a different attitude toward their commodification. Instead of speaking in terms of the opportunity their employer is providing them, they talk about what they are providing their employer. Evelyn Diaz, similar to August Calvo, works at a small Midwestern university. Different from Calvo, though, she is strategic about where she will be commodified and the benefits she expects to gain from the usage of her image by the university. "I know that's part of the capital that I have. I know that I'm a little bit of a token. I'm gonna milk it. I'm going to use it, be strategic about it. I just feel like academia is a game, and you just have to use whatever extra tools you can use to level up. And so if that's the game, I'm just gonna play it and get paid. If it wasn't me, it would be somebody else." Diaz views diversity as a resource. She provides to her university the ability to appear diverse, and she expects to be compensated for it.

Alma Mar was drawn to a regional university in the upper Midwest because of the lucrative startup funds she was offered for her research. Once there, she learned about the other employees of color who had come and gone before her. Because of the university's need to protect its image, she recognizes that the departures of professors of color before her have given her the upper hand. She points out, "So, there's a very queer, different type of power that I've gained, and I think because they're really afraid of the fourth Brown woman in the last ten years to leave. So being able to ask for certain issues has been easier. It's been easier to be more vocal. It's been very interesting to navigate."

One of the places where Mar was more vocal was speaking up about racist comments. Early during her time in the department, and in the middle of a diversity training, one of Mar's colleagues said to her, "Oh well, seeing that you have been hired for diversity." Mar's response was immediate. "And I'm like, did you just . . . ? And I just snapped. I was like, 'I didn't know you were my boss. I should go ahead and start asking you for stuff now. I thought it was so-and-so.' And I saw him tense up." Apparently, Mar hit a nerve because her colleague had tried and failed to become chair of the department.

Mar's confidence derived from her university's need to keep her. It was evident in how she addressed this incident with her vice-chair. "So, I went to the VC, and I'm like, look, you're here thinking you need diversity in your campus and stuff like that. I'm letting you know now. I'm gonna bite back and I'm gonna go ahead and snap back. I'm from the East Coast. And that was totally inappropriate." When I asked her how she had the courage to address the situation head-on, she again mentions her university's track record with women of color.

> I'm on my prime AP [assistant professor] years. I could go ahead and get another job. But I feel like I have the courage to say that because a lot of people have left. There's four people have left before and stuff like that. And it looks so bad in that department, in a university that claims to have the most diverse body and 28 percent women of color in their student body. So, it doesn't look very good. It would look really bad if I didn't get [tenure]. They'll be like, "She didn't get tenure, and yet she got this grant on her first year, and she had this, and she did all of this." Like it would just look so weird. It's like, well, there is a reason why there's a lot of women of color leaving, look at this. So, I feel like I have that courage and I'm in this very interesting position. But if it didn't happen like that, I would be quiet and do my work.

Not only did Mar have the confidence to address her treatment, the position of the department also allows her a different level of power over her identity. When she first showed up at the university, she dressed in a demurer fashion. The power afford by the university's need for diversity has allowed her to take back her preferred style of dress. "If you feel like you want to go ahead and speak up on something, do it, because right now you can. It's not gonna affect your status. I'm back with my hoops. I'm back with my really pink, bright lipstick. I don't care anymore."

Seeing diversity as resource also gives employees the means to strategically reject their commodification. Employees pushed back when doing additional labor for the sake of their employer would not benefit them or the constituencies they care about. An Asian American assistant professor in the South regularly provides mentorship to students of color and designs her classes around their concerns. Recently, her university decided to undertake a diversity initiative and she was asked to provide data on her diversity work as evidence of what the university was doing. She refused, saying, "And now I'm supposed to compile data so that the university can see and quantify that we're doing things about diversity? I've been doing this for years and no one seemed to care until now. I was like, 'No, I'm not giving you this. You need to do better.'" Through her refusal, this professor retains a level of power over her labor and time. She will continue doing the work of diversity, but not for the university's sake. It is an act of resistance that rejects commodification. As she said, "I've also been resisting in other ways. I'm not going to be your token person of color to say, see, look, we're addressing diversity."

Another assistant professor used diversity as resource in negotiating her contract. As a result, she was able to push back against some of the racialized labor she would be asked to do by requiring additional funding up front. This leverage was created by her university's reputational needs. "I knew because the university is trying to be nationally recognized and ranked that they're committed to diversifying, that would put me in a good place as far as negotiating my contract. It did actually help me because I was able to make a case: you don't have anyone here, so what are you going to do to make sure that I come?" Because she would be one of very few Black professors on a campus with racial issues, this professor was able to ask for and receive a higher salary than the standard offer. She was also able to negotiate being protected from committee service during her first two years.

A Black pastor on the West Coast was another employee able to use diversity as resource. Recognizing that the church needed him more than they needed his white counterparts for their image, he was able to gain a sense of power relative to his peers. His power came from a relative scarcity of Black pastors happy to work for his particular church. "As a Black pastor, you're not just another white boy; white boys are disposable. There's just not a shortage of those guys. I knew that, and they knew I knew. I made sure you're going to handle me in in a particular type of way." This pastor saw his white counterparts come and go while he was able to remain in his position. Although he still experienced some difficulties working for the church, he was able to parlay this sense of power into a position at a branch campus that he operated with relative autonomy.

When I spoke with a diversity consultant working for a Black-owned firm, Lawrence Harvey, he affirmed diversity as resource as a necessary step toward creating greater racial equity. His philosophy was that people of color in diverse organizations should leverage their racial capital for long-term collective gains. The ability to do this, he argued, was much more available than the prospect of wholesale change in the racial hierarchy. Harvey's stated goal of having people of color hired by diverse organizations is "getting the resources to establish our autonomy, and keeping our feet in the spaces that we make it into." By doing so, people of color could continue to work toward racial equity. He recounted:

> I was just talking to a brother who works for Bain [& Company] and I could hear the stress coming out of him, you know, you got to stay in those majority white spaces, and you got to be the diversity guy for this university or the chief diversity person for that organization. They brought you in mostly for window dressing. In most cases, even if some people on the team wanted you there for substantive reasons, they still got to battle the ones who don't. Nobody's gonna hire my company to put them out of a job. No biped male CEO's doing that. Nor is he hiring us so he can create a co-CEO position occupied by someone who fits a diversity criterion. It's not why we're here. And so, you have to think in terms of, what can I do with these resources? And it's not just money, right? It's access to networks, it's access to those people who do give a flying farfegnugen . . .

After years of work in diversity, equity, and inclusion roles, Harvey has recognized success is not getting the role but getting resources out of the role. While a diversity consultant may never get the power to make substantive change, they will receive a substantial paycheck and connections to people who may be able to make change in other spheres. In this situation, the endgame is to focus on what can be done with those resources. He continued, "We've got to be about plugging people into networks and getting our people the jobs that pay you well enough to not only meet your needs and your family's needs, but to actually be able to channel resources into community development. That is what we need to be doing in these spaces."

Recognizing that it would be unlikely for any organization to promote diversity to the extent that it threatens people already in power, the soundest strategy, Harvey reasoned, is to use the space afforded strategically. This involves using the job afforded by diversity both to achieve personal financial success and to engage in community uplift. When diversity becomes resource, it is not just about this opportunity, but the one after, and the one after that, generated by a foot in the door. Through community development and reinvestment, then, providing diversity to majority white spaces ceases being the only opportunity and becomes the first of many.

Harvey expects that anything folks of color gain from diversity will not come at the expense of whites. He clearly states that diversity consultants are not there to supplant white CEOs but to support them. Diversity as resource gives financial remuneration and networks to people of color while giving white organizations the window dressing needed to be successful—neither of which threatens existing positions of power.

Harvey's view reflects the principle of *interest convergence* formulated by legal scholar Derrick Bell.[22] Interest convergence states that policies ostensibly promoting the advances for people of color will only be enacted when they benefit middle- and upper-class whites. Looking at the desegregation of schools, for example, Bell's principle pointed to the need of the United States to maintain its reputation in the face of Communism, among other reasons, rather than a new sense of fairness toward Black people. Interest convergence is only a temporary win / win. When whites' interests are no longer served, energies toward advances for people of color dissipate. As a case in point, schools are now as racially segregated as they were in the 1960s, concentrating Black students in high-poverty schools.[23] In another example, cuts in positions related to diversity at the University of Texas, Austin, have resulted in disproportionate firings of Black staffers, who made up one-third of the cuts while only comprising 7 percent of the workforce.[24] Because the gains of diversity as resource are temporary, Harvey is wise to encourage people of color to reinvest into community-based solutions not solely dependent on white institutions.

Conceptualizing diversity as resource is not simply a matter of choice and perspective. Whether diversity is resource or merely opportunity is an illustration of resource dependence theory. According to sociologists Jeffrey Pfeffer and Gerald R. Salancik, organizations attempt to reduce all others' power over them, often attempting to increase their own power over others.[25] The power of employees of color is limited by their position in the racial hierarchy, pervasive hiring discrimination, and lack of access to positions of power in organizational leadership. As a result, the ability of any one employee of color to limit their own commodification is small. Employees of color who do not meet the organizations' needs can be relatively easily replaced.

Diversity as resource, however, appears in situations where the power shifts somewhat in the employee's favor. This happens because the racial capital required by the organization becomes concentrated in an individual. With this concentration of resource comes a concentration of power.[26] As a result, the organization has greater dependency on specific employees of color rather than a generalized need for racial capital. As with Mar's case above, this can occur when one person's outcomes represent the legitimacy of an organization as related to diversity, usually because of past failures in that arena. Another way this happens is that limited labor supply enables well-qualified employees of color to have more choice in where and how they work.

Benefiting from a limited labor supply is Clayton Hudson, a Black tech employee in the south-central portion of the country. Unlike almost any employee I spoke with, he had a rigorous process for vetting companies that he would work for and had already moved companies several times as organizations failed his test. He explained to me, "I only work for certain companies. I look at history. Do they have any bad layoffs? Is there diversity or how is it that there isn't diversity? I'll look if there are women in leadership positions or is the company aware of social issues. Are they overworking you and stuff like that?"

Although his current company only boasted 5 percent Black workers, Hudson enjoyed the working environment, felt as though he could be himself, and appreciated the CEO's response after George Floyd was murdered in the summer of 2020. When I asked him why he had the confidence to make good work environment a nonnegotiable for him, he pointed to his status as an in-demand worker. "I think in technology there is a demand, so I think it works out in my case. In some people's careers, you may not have that. You may not be able to go to another company because there's only this amount of jobs available for this given position. So, I am aware of these things. If you're in high demand, you can kind of have a little bit more control."

Clearly, this matter of labor supply and demand is not racially specific and affects all employees. However, in the case of employees of color, additional leverage becomes critical. Having the power to minimize the heavy work demands, threatened legitimacy, and subjugated identity that comes with commodification could result in a markedly improved work environment with long-term consequences for retention and advancement.

Diversity is a critical resource. When dependence on one specific employee increases or labor is scarce, employees of color can use diversity as a resource. In other cases, it remains opportunity—opportunity created by a generalized value for diversity that may translate to a job but not to personal power. When diversity is opportunity, people of color remain interchangeable and easily replaced, limiting their ability to change the environment around them.[27] Furthermore, even when diversity is resource, any power achieved is often ephemeral: it depends on the needs of white majority organizations, which can shift at any time. As a result, both these components of diversity ideology are responses to the broader landscape rather than preferred choices. It is still true that people would much rather be valued for their holistic selves than their racial identity.

Lifting as You Climb, No Matter What

Regarding these three tenets of diversity ideology, I didn't have a single employee of color who rejected diversity as philanthropy. Whether their organizational situation otherwise made diversity a resource or an opportunity, each employee concluded that they should work for constituencies of color despite the toll to themselves. For example, Calvo, the professor who was hired because of a racist incident on campus, doesn't take this opportunity and only maximize gains for himself. Instead, with his foot in the door, he turns around to give uncompensated labor to the students who protested to get him hired. Mar, who put back on her pink lipstick and hoop earrings, didn't just empower herself through diversity as resource; she reached students in the process, allowing them to express their identity in a more open way. She said proudly, "I saw the reactions from the students of color in my class, like another student told me, 'Oh, did you see so-and-so, she's back wearing her box braids. She really went back to her Blackness ever since you came here.'" Rejecting the simple idea of being entrepreneurs of themselves, only for themselves, employees of color in my sample universally use diversity to improve gains for the constituencies they care about.

It is important to note that employees of color do not think philanthropically out of an abundance of time and resources but rather out of lack. These employees already remark that they are doing two jobs to white employees' one because of the additional labor commodification extracts. Offering their time and attention to constituencies of color then comes on top of impromptu appearances at meetings to display a nonwhite face. Because employees of color embrace diversity as philanthropy, they are in the position of having to succeed at two jobs plus a side hustle: the job they were hired for, their responsibilities as a commodity, and the philanthropic work they cannot give up.

By undergirding institutions that are poorly designed for people of color, these employees allow their employers to continue engaging in racial outsourcing. Arguably without uncompensated support for employees and constituents of color in their organizations, there would be a smaller base of minoritized people who would remain. The employees I spoke with were not unaware of the organizational benefit they contribute, even as they focus on benefits to the people they serve. As one put it in the quote that gave this chapter its title, "I'm not improving the white space for the white people. I'm improving it for us. And yes, they benefit from it in some ways, but I know that we have to [do this work] in order for us to do the things that need to be done in the next generation and next generation." Despite this justification, diversity as philanthropy allows organizations to remain unchanged at their core while monopolizing the capacities of employees of color. As a consequence, this tenet of diversity ideology ultimately contributes to racial inequality.

Through the diversity ideology of white people and institutions, "white people who consider themselves progressive and perhaps even antiracist enact practices and policies that perpetuate systemic whiteness."[28] This happens because of the value diversity extracts from people of color and redistributes to white people and institutions. In like manner, employees of color reinforce current racial hierarchies through their diversity ideology. By supporting constituencies of color within diverse organizations, employees of color provide the necessary racial equity labor to maintain the racial outsourcing that ultimately disadvantages them. Employees of color attempt to compensate for an inequitable racial structure and end up more disadvantaged by that very same structure by a deficit of time and energy for career advancement. However, as sociologist Tressie McMillan Cottom's pointed statement in the epigraph to the chapter emphasizes, their ability to make the changes they'd like to see is limited while the potential for harm to their lives and careers is great.[29] Even when leveraging their racial capital for financial gain, employees of color are ultimately philanthropists who give more than they get in return.

6 *Making Diversity the Only Option*

It feels like an all-day cheat day to be only in Black spaces. I only talk to Black people. I only work on Black things. All the shows I'm watching, all the books. It's just like all Black everything. And if it's not Black, it's people of color, and it feels like, like summertime; just like ice cream after dinner.

NICHOLE HILL, producer

When Pastor Bryce Rhodes saw his soon-to-be mentor preach for the first time, he was awestruck. "When I saw this church and heard him preach, I was just like, Yo, this dude looks like me. And I guess he goes to seminary, and this is what seminary produces. And all of these people in here, especially these white people are listening to him and like, they following him. I need to do that." Seeing that level of respect and admiration afforded to a Black preacher by whites was unheard of in Rhodes's experience. Pastor Rhodes was all in. He enrolled in seminary, joined the same church where he met his mentor, and tried to replicate this status come-up in his own ministry career.

Status denotes the amount of respect, honor, and deference people receive from others.[1] One way to attain status is to join certain workplaces—workplaces with high levels of resources and prestige that can increase the status of those associated with them. Status can also be gained in other organizations related to employment, including the university one attends or the clubs one belongs to. Status is often in short supply for people of color, especially Black and Latino/a people who receive less deference and honor than whites because of racism. So, a workplace offering the potential for higher status is especially temping for minoritized people. This is the temptation that lured Pastor Rhodes, the Black Southern megachurch pastor, whose stress and disillusionment I discuss in chapter 3, from a Black church to a diverse (majority white) one.

In this chapter, I show how the prestige of organizations, their component parts, and processes and people associated with the term "professional" play an outsized role in the workplaces people of color choose to join. This would be fine if prestige were race neutral; however, prestige is intimately connected to racial groups.[2] As a result, employees of color seeking prestige in work are likely to be shunted into majority white organizations. This diminished agency appears in the jobs accepted by and expected behavior of employees of color. By attracting or channeling employees of color into positions that are disadvantageous to their well-being, organizations' rankings and practices reinforce racial inequality.

Status Lift and Letdown

Another Black pastor who, like Rhodes, chose employment based on status, worked at a church among the thirty largest in America. He commented that although his employment there was harmful to him, it helped him make connections: "I didn't want to bring diversity, but it didn't hurt that I was functioning in this organization, that I was attached to it in some way. And I used that. It hurt internally, but externally, it put you on an upwardly mobile trajectory." Just being able to name-drop this church opened doors for him in ministry and fundraising. Despite those advantages, this pastor now admits he was playing a losing game and that the church came out on top. "And these churches ultimately leverage you. You know, it's not a win-win because they're not going to change."

Pastor Rhodes did experience a bit of the increase in status he hoped for, graduating seminary and preaching at the church for several years as a resident, a pastoral position designed for training new ministers. He did well and was promised a permanent position at one of the campus sites his church was opening. In the end, however, Rhodes's story ended like many others in this book: painfully. In Rhodes's case, he publicly discovered the promised role would not materialize. "[The pastor] brings me out on stage. And then he says, 'Man, we would love to keep this brother on staff but you know, it's just crazy. So, in a few months, this brother is gonna need a job. So, someone hire him.'" No one did. Rhodes found himself unemployed with a newborn daughter.

Rhodes was not only let go, but also felt abandoned. When he started his own church, this previous church did not contribute financially toward his new venture, as would be typical in conservative Protestant circles. Established churches often play a "parent church" role to new start-ups, helping with advice and funds. Rhodes received nothing. "So, they don't give me a dollar. I'm okay; I've gotten a lot of what I needed. But there are scars from that." This lack of care did not keep the established church from taking credit for Rhodes's accomplishments, continuing the diversity display even after Rhodes had departed. They frame themselves as a church that trains successful Black ministers, using the pastors they have let go as evidence. Because of how his tenure at the church ended, Pastor Rhodes now describes the desire for status that brought him into this environment as a "trap."

After he was let go from his diverse church, Rhodes found solace and healing within the Black church. "[The Lord] gave me a soft space to land in a Black church, and it was everything I needed. I learned how to pastor in a Black church. I learned how to receive love in a Black church. I was around my people; I could be freely myself to some degree." In the process of this healing, Rhodes also undid some of the theological leanings that he developed within his previous church. "One of the church mothers says, 'Son, I've been a Christian longer than you've been alive. What you saying ain't new. We been hearing that. Don't you bring them white theologians up here.'" Rhodes learned that the Black church had wisdom he previously missed. As it turns out, Black church mothers weren't ignorant of white theologians; they already knew enough to know they were not impressed by them.

Diverse or Majority-Minority?

The difference in status between Rhodes's diverse church and his Black one exists because of how these two churches are racialized. Sociologist Victor Ray theorizes that organizations, like people, are viewed differently based on the racial groups that they are associated with.[3] Racialization extends the meaning of race and its hierarchies from people to things, including organizations. Organizations that are viewed as whiter, such as organizations termed "diverse," will receive additional resources and esteem as compared to organizations that are associated with people of color.[4] The respect and admiration Rhodes sought by being part of his mentor's church was made possible by the church's association with diversity.

There is a bit of irony here, in that the designation "diverse" signals the presence of at least some people of color, but allows racialization as white, at least up to a point. Diversity tends to be built around inviting people of color into white organizations rather than the other way around.[5] Simply calling an organization "diverse" emphasizes a white normative center.[6] This expectation frames whites as the hosts and people of color as the guests. That's why, in spaces routinely called diverse, whiteness is the standard that diversity is measured against. Whiteness is not simply about white people. It is an ideology that creates the category of white people, privileging and guarding membership to that group, while classifying everyone else as a racial other.[7] So much so that people of color have often been called "diverse" as a euphemism.[8] This euphemism makes no sense unless you ask, diverse as compared to whom? Diverse organizations get a status bump because of their association with whiteness when compared to majority-minority organizations. Majority-minority organizations are those in which people of color are in the majority, hold leadership positions, and structure how the organization is run. Diverse organizations also get an additional benefit of being associated with the right sort of middle-class, nonracist whiteness where people of color are present.

The status of diverse organizations underscores that organizations are racialized as white, and therefore mainstream, or something else, based on a number of factors that go beyond simple demographics. Some organizations' racial assignments are obvious; in the case of Historically Black Colleges and Universities (HBCUs), their designation aligns with their racial status. Organizations obviously marked with a racial status are often stigmatized as a result of it. By contrast, organizations that are considered "white" are mostly left unmarked—a reflection of how white is standard and unnamed in other arenas as well.

But just being unmarked is not enough to keep an organization safe from racial stigma. Organizations can still be associated with people of color based on a number of factors including how they operate, who leads them, and their neighborhood. Their racialization can mean the difference between success and failure. In a study I did on multiracial churches with sociologists Christopher Munn and Korie Little Edwards, we compared a multiracial church termed diverse to a similar church characterized as Black.[9] Today, only the diverse church is still open. These churches were located in the same city, within fifteen minutes of each other; had nearly identical donations from members; and were part of the same religious tradition. What's more, both churches had nearly the same number of folks of color! The two things that shifted the churches' racial designations were the race of the leader and the neighborhood of the church. While the white-led, diverse church in the gentrifying neighborhood earned enough external donations to survive, the "Black" church ended up closing. The white pastor who led the diverse church explicitly cultivated diversity in the church's appeals for funds, separating himself rhetorically from the other church, which he rightly assumed would fail.

The precarity of racial assignment for organizations means that they have to guard their status. Too much demographic change and an organization can incur racial stigma. Employment scholar Sarah Damaske's study of a university showed how job recruiters stopped visiting the school as the demographic shifted to 90 percent Black and Latino/a students.[10] Pastors, too, are apprehensive if their congregations shift too far from a white majority. One East Coast lead pastor even interrogated his associate pastor as to why so many Black congregants were showing up. "He's like, 'I'm not African American. I don't preach Black. Everybody knows I'm Republican. I'm always talking about how I love George Bush and doing George Bush impersonations.'" The pastor was happy to welcome a diverse congregation, but not when it threatened to become a majority Black one. He felt he was giving out a sufficient nod to whiteness in the form of political speech but was dismayed that too many Black congregants kept showing up.

Status by Association

The status of an organization does not just affect the organization but also the people associated with it.[11] When a person is associated with a high-status organization, their status receives a boost as a result. This status boost also applies when the status is generated by racialization, providing an additional incentive for people of color to join organizations that are deemed as diverse rather than majority-minority. For Pastor Rhodes, this meant that a white-led, diverse church was perceived as more advantageous than a Black church where he felt most at home.

The employees I spoke with well understood how organizations affected their status. One assistant professor in a prestigious Northeastern institution remarked how opportunities for faculty of color are truncated by virtue of the schools they are associated with. When I asked him about improving equity for faculty of color, he commented, "I think the piece that might be left out or missed is that there are very talented faculty of color that don't come from elite institutions." A corporate employee within a hospital system remarked the same about the opportunities opened by certain medical schools: "In this world of physicians, it's about the medical school that you went to. People get so caught up in that. And if you went to an HBCU that has a medical school, you know, maybe you're not going to be looked at [the same] as the student that came out of this prestigious, medical school, all white." Note here the use of adjectives "elite" or "prestigious," which are not explicitly racial but are used to denote schools associated with white faculty or doctors. The implication is that the people receiving the best opportunities will not be associated with schools that people of color come from.

In justifying the status decrement charged to organizations associated with people of color, employees often explained that white organizations represent the "real world" and majority-minority organizations occupy an alternate reality. A Black employee for a Mid-Atlantic pharmacy company told me that her success would be limited by what she was able to learn from an HBCU about her future work environments. Furthermore, she credits being able to have professional conversations to her familiarity with white people.

I wasn't thinking about HBCUs because the real world is not what HBCUs look like. And as much as I know I would really enjoy it, I'm trying to prepare myself for the fact that I know when I'm working, I most likely won't be the majority. I knew that the real world was not like this. You know, those professional conversations when you're trying to leverage your career, it's different if the person was Black versus if it was a white person. [Life] is almost like an obstacle course for Black people. And each obstacle is a very big one that some people aren't able to cross, and some people are able to cross. In college, those experiences that I learned have really helped me.

So, what was the "experience" that she couldn't learn at an HBCU? Well, as it turns out, it is how to deal with racism. Rather than lessons from classes, or the rules to water polo, this employee learned how to advocate for herself and her classmates after being harassed multiple times on campus. She learned how to avoid campus security and curry favor with the dean when she was mistreated. That dealing with racism outranks other skills needed is quite a sad commentary on the world of work encountered by employees of color.

It may be common knowledge that HBCUs disadvantage students in the real world, but like much common knowledge this too is mostly false. Although HBCU graduates do experience stigma concerning their schools, they achieve success in spite of it. HBCUs have been extremely effective for their core constituency, providing Black students a greater sense of belonging, higher career aspirations, and a greater likelihood of postsecondary enrollment relative to predominantly white institutions.[12] HBCUs may even improve the health of graduates years later, as they are less likely to develop health problems in midlife.[13] Despite these benefits of HBCUs, students are convinced instead to attend schools that are viewed as diverse to hitch their status to majority white institutions. To quote Pastor Rhodes, this seems like a "trap" indeed.

Making Diversity the Only Choice

The status difference between unmarked, predominantly white organizations and stigmatized majority-minority ones is complicit in creating the costs of diversity. Employees of color, like those quoted above, are drawn to organizations promoting diversity because of what they believe these organizations will afford them in terms of personal advancement, advancement that didn't seem possible through organizations that were stigmatized by race. These employees' understandings even lead them to ignore evidence to the contrary; for example, that HBCUs could be better for long-term success than predominantly white universities. In the case of Pastor Rhodes, it was ultimately the Black church where he was restored to mental health, regained his confidence for leadership, and from which he was able to go on to lead his own church. Yet, he could not appreciate what the Black church had to offer until the status boost expected from the diverse church lost its luster. By this time, Pastor Rhodes experienced significant trauma from his employment.

The racialization of organizations limits agency.[14] When people of color seek employment, they do so based on the resources available to potential employers based on their status. Higher levels of resourcing and status can make organizations promoting diversity go from being framed as one option among many to the only smart option. As a result, employees of color face additional pressure to opt into these workplaces only to later experience the personal and professional hardships described in chapters 2 and 3.

White Normativity

Some hardships for employees of color in diverse workplaces derive from the racial norms of these spaces. For evidence that racial norms exist, picture an all-Black church in your head, if not from life experience, maybe from TV portrayals or something you have read in a book. Now picture a majority white church in your head. You probably note some clear distinctions between the two in terms of music, preaching style, and even the general culture reflected by each. Instead of operating in a middle space between these two norms, diverse churches exhibit white normativity by adopting the same worship practices used in majority white churches.[15] They can be marked by a "religion of whiteness" when they accept ideologies and beliefs that privilege whites as their commonsense understanding of how things should be.[16] White normativity sets whiteness as the standard by which all others are measured.[17] When this happens, white cultural norms and experiences are treated as ordinary while excluding or denigrating the norms of other groups.

When Pastor Rhodes joined the church that portrayed itself as diverse, he found that they elevated a preaching style oriented around white preachers and audiences. "So, it felt like the 'white way.' Like this more lecture-style sermon is somehow better," Pastor Rhodes reported. "Because of that, it makes Black preachers' sermons and methods less-than." Being a great preacher in Rhodes's context meant following a certain pattern of preaching that was not typical in Black churches but seen as standard in white ones. It meant quoting prominent white theologians. This caused Rhodes to denigrate the Black Church and aspects associated with it. "I was a jerk because I learned all of these things that I didn't know. And I thought people in Black churches didn't [know]."

Music is another area in which diverse churches reject styles associated with Black churches in favor of those associated with white ones. One Black West Coast pastor attempted to introduce more gospel music to his church, only to be met with multiple excuses as to why that was not possible. "I said, 'Hey, it'd be great to have some songs sung by African Americans in the worship.' The response was, 'Well, you know, most African Americans don't know how to read music, and they play by ear. We probably can't get the sheet music.' So, I got all the sheet music and gave it to them, and then it was 'Oh, the gospel music is just too hard.' And I found out they were just playing chords."

In this case, Black religious music was alternatively stigmatized as lacking the normative format—sheet music—to become useful to the church, then fetishized as being too complicated. This quick shift in the excuses for not introducing new music styles seemed less than genuine, even more so because the musicians at the church in question were not playing sheet music in the first place, just chord charts. These objections allowed the church to maintain musical styles oriented around white congregants, perpetuating the whiteness of the space. Through maneuvers like these, not only do organizations promoting diversity operate on white normativity, they also reinforce it.

Racialized Departments and Jobs

Organizations experience racial status differences, and so do their component parts. So, when people of color join an organization that is unmarked by racial stigma, the specific department they are assigned to may still be. Employees of color can be concentrated in niche positions considered outside of the primary functions of their organization.[18] When this occurs, it can be easy to remove resources from these areas, leaving employees of color at a disadvantage.

One way that this racialized structure was evident was in the academic departments where people of color were concentrated. Employees reported departments such as Ethnic Studies experiencing disadvantages in terms of resources and perceived necessity. When I asked what being part of a university that portrays itself as diverse costs employees of color, a Latino assistant professor specifically mentioned the level of resources in a department associated with Latino/as. "It is the uncertainty I know that my colleagues and Latino Studies exists in. The president announced that there was going to be reprioritization of programs. If I don't make a strong enough case for what I do and show that what I do is actually important, it's easy for my tenure file to be rejected." Beyond the pressure to deliver great scholarship, professors in departments associated with people of color also have to prove that their work is important, often in the face of cutbacks. Another professor spoke of her department this way: "You know, we joke with each other, we call it the academic ghetto. We call it an academic ghetto because our building is so old. All of the area studies, all of the minority departments are on the same floor. And so, it's like, it's crappy, but it's our crap. It's our crap. It's ours." Gratitude at having a department at all mentally counteracts the underresourcing and uncertainty this scholar experiences. But it does not mitigate the racialized disadvantages in resources and esteem that these departments absorb.

Some academic departments focused on people of color are not departments at all, but concentrations. The lower levels of resources assigned to these programs create additional stress for professors of color who are often assigned to a home department and also required to teach in an ethnic-specific program. The additional work necessitated by this dynamic doesn't always become apparent to new professors until after they are hired.

And as I did more research about cluster hires in general, I realized that this is something that a lot of faculty of color get sucked into. Because, historically, the disciplines are very white, and you have this fight for ethnic studies in the university. And so, they created a separate program, around Black Studies, Asian Studies, Latinx studies, whatever. And then there's always this vying for place and power, position and resources between the disciplines and those programs. And so, you know, faculty of color get kind of thrown into that mix. That's something I didn't know. Of course, no one explained that to me during the interview process. It's something I had to navigate once I got the job.

Academic departments and programs focused on people of color, while necessary to university reputations, are not well resourced relative to other departments. This internal status difference has ripple effects for the faculty of color associated with them, resulting in additional work demands and a harder road toward tenure.

Professional (White)

After graduating from a Hispanic-serving institution, Carmen Hernández was specifically hired by her radio station because they needed a Spanish-speaking Latina for the market. In Hernández's job, she was on-air talent for both a Spanish-language and white-contemporary music station. While she was invited to be herself as long as she was on the Spanish-language station, she was limited in what she could do on the white station. "I was told to be very happy and smiling and sound very much not like myself. I sound naturally more laid back, more chill. A lot of Spanglish. My friends hear me on the radio; they're like 'Who is that? Like, you sound super white,' and deep down I'm like, 'Oh, why, I can't be myself even in my job,' you know?"

Hernández played recordings of her work for the two sessions, and I agreed with her friends' perspective. The recording for the white station sounded nothing like the person I had spoken with for the previous hour and a half. Although Hernández would love to sound more like herself, any deviation from this put-upon, "white" voice lands her in the manager's office.

In speaking about how she had to change her voice based on which station she was working for, Hernández used the word "professional." When I asked if she was made to feel that her white voice was her professional voice, she responded, "Yeah, definitely. I hate that. But yes. That's just how I was trained. I hate that I had to say white is synonymous to being professional which is like no, I need to unlearn everything I've ever learned in my life." Hernandez colorfully described this unlearning process as having a "white man in her head" that she has to silence constantly. Through her work experiences, Hernández was taught to valorize the sort of speech that was valued by a white station as professional, positioning her speech on the Spanish-language station in opposition to this professional norm. In this way, Hernández was made to feel that there was something less than professional about her, especially if she were to be herself. Through their assessments of her work, Hernández's station perpetuated the idea that white-normative speech patterns were more desirable than others, even if coming from the mouth of an employee of color.

Professional is a term laden with positive value; who doesn't want to be professional? Well, as it turns out, not everyone can be. Communication scholars George Cheney and Karen Lee Ashcraft find that professionalism is used to disparage certain individuals or groups for not meeting standards of whiteness or maleness: "The idea of professionalism lurks as a means of shaping, containing, and legitimizing appearance, decorum, behavior, and attitude."[19] It thereby constrains the acceptable boundaries of workplace behaviors in ways correlated more with personal characteristics than with job performance. This is in part because the development of the "professional" was a process that intentionally excluded women and people of color as other so as to protect the status and remuneration of jobs associated with white men.[20] The seemingly neutral language of "professional" allows organizations to reinforce white racial norms in their ways of operation and in their expectations of employees of color. These expectations reinforce racial hierarchies by reshaping or rejecting employees of color.

Comportment consistent with the professional self also means abandoning other cultural norms. For one assistant professor, it changed the way he interacted with other Latino/as. Even when no one else was present to witness his behavior, the organizational expectations constrained his behavior. When I asked what professional meant for him, he offered this example of changing his actions even around those who share his culture:

So, at home, when we meet someone from a different gender, when we say hi, we kiss each other on the cheek. That's it. It's cultural. But you know expectations of boundaries and whatever and then sort of processing that you can't do that. Right? So, the professional self always extends the hand no matter what. And even with people of my own culture. So, I have one of my students from home, and his parents came and visited. They came to my office. Under normal circumstances, I would have given the mom a kiss on the cheek. Like that's what you do. Even though we were in my office, there was no one else. Mm hmm. You extend the hand. And it's now become so ingrained that you become someone else. You lose that part of yourself.

Professionalization for those who do not meet the standards of whiteness or maleness will demand forsaking a part of oneself. Whether it is in their voice, their customs of greeting, their preferred vernacular, their hairstyle or dress, employees of color are forced to give up bits and pieces of themselves every time they arrive at the office. This assimilation to professional norms imbued with whiteness may cause employees of color to feel as though they are losing themselves.

Ideas of professionalism can extend from comportment to the type of work done in a given job. Those who fall short of "professional" because their work focuses on marginalized groups may be excluded from legitimate membership in their profession altogether. Above, I relayed how Pastor Rhodes was driven toward white theologians in his preaching. This is not simply a privileging of white theologians, but a reflection that white religious writers are called *theologians* while writers of other races are classified differently.[21] An Asian American pastor shared with me how the established theological canon slowed his process of understanding the Christian Bible's "power and status dynamics." He mentioned, "I asked a prominent Christian leader, 'Can you share with me some theologians of color?' And she's like, 'It's crazy how you're even saying that statement. There are theologians in the wide world, but if I list these names, people won't look at them as theologians. They'll be seen as activists, or that they're just simply writers.'" Authors whose writings interrogated ideas of status, race, and how power differences could be important to religion were thereby marginalized in the study of theology. By demeaning these ideas, examinations of the dominance that benefits white people and institutions are excluded from the training of pastors. What it means to be professional excludes critical examinations of whiteness; ask any employee who has ever complained about workplace discrimination too forcefully.

The exclusion of topics associated with privilege and power also applies in the academic realm. One professor expressed that she did not feel her colleagues considered her equally part of their field because of her area of focus. "I feel like my very existence as a professor is based on white folks feeling like they're doing a good job. I don't feel deep in my spirit and soul that they think I'm a scientist like they are, right? I just think they think we're doing different things and that it's important to have me there so that they can feel good about this 'diversity mission.'" Because her scholarship focused on racial issues instead of what some scholars saw as mainstream concerns, she felt excluded from what made a scientist a scientist from the perspective of her peers.

Professional (White) Organizations

In addition to the restrictions on individuals' behavior and area of focus, there are restrictions on organizations that want to be viewed as professional. Organizations deemed professional exhibit remarkable similarity in form, shape, and structure. Most people assume that is because the practices they have adopted are most efficient. This is simply how a business plan, or sermon, or course catalog is best done, right? Wrong. As it turns out, the copycat behavior of organizations is created through the process of institutional isomorphism, coined by sociologists Paul DiMaggio and Walter Powell.[22] Organizations that are acted on by similar forces in their broader environment are pushed to become similar in operation, whether or not the way that they operate is most efficient or effective. Institutional pressures that create this effect include coercive pressure to meet the professional standards of the field, normative pressure to gain legitimacy, and mimetic pressure to copy other organizations so as to limit uncertainty.

While institutional isomorphism has traditionally been styled as a racially neutral process, recent investigations have shown that standards do not spread in the same ways depending on how they are racialized. Sociologist Laura Garbes has coined the term *white institutional isomorphism* to show the way that race matters for the diffusion of organizational models.[23] In her study on the birth of National Public Radio (NPR), she found that the founders exhibited coercive rule-making that excluded nonwhite stations from becoming member stations based on technical standards. She also found that normative standards in recruiting excluded radio personalities of color from being hired. Finally mimetic pressure caused NPR to copy types of shows that were generally understood to be of interest to a mainstream (white) audience. These choices to align with professional standards all reinforced white racial norms, ignored alternative models, and created pervasive racial inequality within public radio that persists today.

Even organizations that initially escape the draw of white organizational norms may be drawn into them as they mature. As an example of how this isomorphism occurs for churches, Alejandra Castillo, who we met back in chapter 2, was an essential part of founding a diverse church in a small Southern city. The church draws people of many nations despite being located in a notoriously segregated region. At first, she was encouraged by the voice she was given in the direction of the church. As the church grew and began to implement models typical of other churches, however, this all began to change.

> I think after five years, that's when there was much more growth than we could handle, and that's when we were like, ahhhh! What happened? We don't have the infrastructure to hold all this together. And I think when I left, maybe there were seven hundred people. When we were smaller, we had just amazing relational intimacy across cultures. It was rich. But then when it starts growing really fast, you know, it is not as intimate. And I know that there's a strict formula like, how do you manage that well? When I left, the church was big and needed more systems and structures to hold it all together. Then sometimes the consequence, the collateral damage of, of enacting systems and structures that are cold, you know, feel less relational; these cookie-cutter systems. My experience, in the beginning, was that I saw those systems and structures that were not [racially] neutral. That system and structure are diseased DNA. Like, no, this is whiteness.

Castillo experienced an organization, which she helped build, being remade according to standards that reflected whiteness. As it grew, the church became a place that she did not recognize as the same organization. The need to manage growth left only certain systems as standard and those systems were imbued with whiteness that changed the character of the church.

A Black pastor in a Midwestern church also expressed frustration with the standard forms of church that his organization utilized. "A lot of the influences that are now impacting us are from white churches. I think that's probably what contributes to it feeling more like a white church. One time I said, 'Hey, how about learning from a church that is Black-led and see what their best practices are?'" When churches borrow from predominantly white churches, it is not as though there are not other possibilities. Black churches make up nearly a quarter of the megachurch category of churches—church with over two thousand attenders—that are considered widely successful. Still, they are not as likely as their white counterparts to have models pervade institutional norms across church types.[24] This difference affects aspects of service from preaching to music to children's ministry. For example, "We have discussions on how you handle babies in service? We are a multiethnic church. This church has their babies in service. But it's, hey, this is how we do it, we're not going to have babies in service. There's not a compromise." Normative standards of how to do church exclude learning from nonwhite congregations.

Constraint

In Zakiya Dalila Harris's debut novel, *The Other Black Girl,* the protagonist faces a choice between being successful and being true to herself. A review of the book frames it this way: "If you choose the first path, as a young Black woman, you may find yourself sublimating your true self—not just style and taste, but the very ideas and principles at your core. If you choose the second path, as a young Black woman, you'll own your identity, but you'll never sit in the corner office—you'll cause too much friction along the way."[25]

This choice is a clear and present reality for the employees I spoke with. Organizations and their component parts are racialized in ways that make status dependent on whiteness. This is particularly true for organizations that market diversity; their ability to profit from racial capital rapidly diminishes if they go from being seen as "diverse" to minority focused.[26] To maintain their status, organizations that want to successfully market diversity must simultaneously attract employees of color and then socialize them into environments centered around white racial norms that, at best, other them and, at worst, denigrate them. For employees of color, then, being successful means going along with this socialization; being true to themselves often means walking away.

The racialization of organizations limits agency and there are a couple of ways to get it back.[27] Naming the racialization of organizations and norms within them is one way to begin replacing whiteness as the standard with something else. Another way is for employees of color to choose majority-minority organizations and workplaces despite those organizations' structural disadvantages. There has been some evidence of this—for example, with high-profile college athletes and stellar scholars like Nikole Hannah-Jones choosing HBCUs. After all, if the possibility of status enhancement from joining a diverse organization is often a "trap," why step into it?

7   Formal Diversity Practices

Like the road to hell, this all started with good intentions. I wanted to open more places and opportunities to people of color! And then it hit me. Like a Molotov cocktail straight to the face. This wasn't my company. I was not the CEO. I didn't own this company. I didn't create the culture. And just like my new hire did not have the power to be themselves at work, I did not have the power to change that reality for us.

BELINDA J. SMITH, marketing professional

In an infamous episode of *The Office*, regional manager Michael Scott implements Diversity Day. Scott's stated purpose for this day was to create an "Oprah moment" and "stir the melting pot."[1] Instead, after Scott crudely mocked an employee's nationality, a Jerry Springer moment surfaced with physical and symbolic violence breaking out.[2] Certainly, the cause of inclusion was not served that day, and neither were employees of color. They were subject to blatant racism in addition to the general discomfort experienced by all.

Fortunately, none of the workplaces represented in this book follow Michael Scott's "Diversity Tomorrow" (because today is almost over) curriculum. But their formal diversity efforts, including trainings and mentoring programs, are often likewise a source of pain for employees of color. The truth is many formal diversity programs result in negative consequences for the hiring, representation, and diversity climate of employees of color.[3] An extensive thirty-year study from sociologists Frank Dobbin and Alexandra Kalev looked at various types of antidiscrimination policies, including diversity training, antiharassment measures, and official grievance processes. Measuring the effects twenty years post-implementation, Dobbin and Kalev find that most programs are correlated with *lower* representation of women and people of color managers. What's more, these programs may be even less effective than their study shows. Diversity scholarship has often looked at the success or failure of diversity strategies using numerical representation as the key outcome.[4] But representation is only one aspect of diversity climate, which also includes employee perceptions of both formal commitments to diversity and informal values.[5] High levels of representation in the absence of a positive climate may be misleading, particularly if this representation is achieved through a revolving door of employees.

Here, I take a slightly different tack to measuring effectiveness by asking employees of color to describe the effectiveness of diversity initiatives. Their accounts focus on formal diversity programs—the things that employers would say they are doing toward diversity—as opposed to the unintended negative effects of diversity discussed in chapters 2 and 3. Each employee was asked what special programs or initiatives their workplace utilized to show concern about diversity. While employees will not have a holistic view of all the initiatives their employers are undertaking, I find that they do have some clear knowledge of and perspective on these programs. The perspectives of employees of color matter for their evaluation of internal legitimacy. When employees see programs that do not help them to be highly resourced and promoted, this undermines their view of workplace legitimacy. Looking at diversity initiatives this way is also an important departure from other studies that have measured the effectiveness of diversity initiatives by focusing on the perceptions of *nontargets*, in this case, white employees.[6] Focusing on nontargets rather than targets perpetuates the idea that employees of color are happy with whatever effort is directed at them. I found this not to be the case.

Nondiscrimination Practices

Scholars have divided types of diversity initiatives into three primary categories: nondiscrimination practices, resource practices, and accountability practices.[7] Nondiscrimination practices are designed to reduce bias in the workplace by ensuring that key elements of employment, including hiring, firing, and promotions, are based on qualifications rather than demographics. The practice in this category that employees of color most frequently mentioned was diversity training. This is not surprising because diversity training is the most common workplace intervention to diminish bias. It is also one of the least effective because of the backlash it generates.[8]

Employees that I spoke with felt backlash from diversity training in a couple of ways. One was in personal hurt from racist attitudes expressed during the training. This was the case for Cadence Coaston. Coaston has moved through a variety of different roles in her company, but her current role is her favorite to date. It involves recruiting Brown and Black high school students for jobs that are entry level but offer tuition benefits for higher education. She also enjoys her job because of the composition of her work team—in Coaston's group, her manager and four of the ten employees are Black women. Having been in corporate work, Coaston is pragmatic about the slights she expects at work as a woman of color. "And I never take it personally, unless you make it personal." But she did take personally what happened at the diversity training in her department.

What hurt Coaston was hearing her white coworkers talk openly about their fear of Black men. She recalled, "There was a ton of conversation. Like, 'Have you been walking down the street and clutched your purse because a Black man was walking towards you.' And all of them have done it." Coaston initially expressed gratitude that her coworkers had the chance to confront their racism, saying, "I like having those conversations because I want people to really hear themselves and understand what's really going on and how not to be that." When I asked her about her own feelings, however, the response was much less positive. She lamented, "You think, heck, are we really still doing this? You would think that we're further along in life and society. That's a disappointment to me." Coaston socialized with her coworkers outside of work, and had even eaten their potato salad, so she took their fears to heart.

While her coworkers had a chance to be introspective about their racial attitudes, Coaston had to experience the racism hidden in the people she works with every day. Interestingly, based on her first comments to me, Coaston would probably have scored this training high on an evaluation simply because of the opportunities it offered to others to confront their racism. This initial positivity ignores the hurt and disappointment she faced. The different response based on the question posed shows that unless employees of color are asked about their own experiences, this information may not be forthcoming. Such diversity trainings are often designed around correcting whites in the group while largely ignoring the impact on employees of color, as was the case here.[9]

Just talking about diversity can put a spotlight on employees of color, resulting in teasing or other insults after a diversity training. After his work unit went through a mandatory implicit bias module, one employee spoke of the unwelcome wisecracks he received. "I've had team members joke about unconscious bias, like, 'Oh, I don't want to unconsciously . . .' like, you know, some stupid joke. So obviously, they're not taking it seriously." In another incident, and as related in chapter 5, Dr. Mar was called a "diversity hire" after her department's diversity training. For employees of color, diversity trainings can result in backlash that makes their workplaces more hostile than they were before the training.

On top of creating backlash, diversity trainings often require additional uncompensated labor from employees of color to occur in the first place. This practice was pervasive across organization types. Just as marketer Belinda J. Smith pointed out in the scathing article quoted in the epigraph, these unofficial tasks come with a great deal of work and little ability to make real change.[10] Churches, universities, and corporations all pushed their employees of color to implement, create, select contractors for, and follow up on diversity training. The assumption becomes that people of color have the know-how to conduct this work even if it is not their area of expertise.[11] One assistant professor was brought on to a committee to lead such a training only to find out that the group she was invited to was entirely Black. "So, the faculty director, he's like, 'I'm all about injustice.' He wanted to do this diversity and inclusion week. But then the committee he brought together, we're only the Black faculty. I wasn't surprised. But I was just like, of course. Got it. You see me as that person, right?" This professor's expertise was STEM rather than race, but she and the other Black faculty were seen as the only people to put together a diversity training for the rest of the group.

Because most churches do not have the resources of a large corporation, often pastors of color must create, as well as deliver, the trainings their employers request. One West Coast pastor did this work for multiple years. "Me and another African American, we did a six- to eight-week teaching series called Cross-Cultural Competence for the church. So, we took each of those groups through the curriculum. After we finished that two-year program, we then created another adult community for those that want to join to learn. So, there's a lot of effort." Stewarding this diversity training year after year became a large part of this pastor's role even though it wasn't what he was explicitly hired to do.

Other times, trainings put the onus on employees of color to display their pain for the education of others. This can retraumatize employees of color, not for their own healing, but to put on display the ugliness of racism for those who have not experienced it. One Black employee in an educational setting was attending a diversity training with his work group about creating brave spaces. One aspect of the training was to ask employees of color to speak up about their mistreatment. When he heard this, the employee raised an objection to the likely result, "I'm like, 'Hi y'all, let's just make sure that we're not asking people of color to do emotional labor.'" The response that this employee received was ironically a request to fix the shortcoming of the training. "And so [the person running the training] goes, 'That's a great point. How will you do that in your classrooms?' She ended up that conversation by saying, 'Don't ask people of color to do labor.' I was just like, but like, but you did that." By bringing up an objection in the training, this employee then also had the responsibility to solve it and provide the solution back to the rest of his team.

A final consequence of diversity training mentioned by employees I spoke with was the frustration of engaging in a program that they know does not work. Many had either seen the research or the consequences of past trainings and were fed up with diversity training as the ready solution. This compounded the threatened legitimacy that employees of color already experience as they know their organizations portray themselves as more concerned with equity than they actually are. One Black assistant professor on the West Coast shared how she had seen trainings over the past fifteen years with no discernible impact. "I'm like we already know that diversity trainings don't work because people are like, 'I have to be here' and bring that attitude of 'I'm only here because I have to be.'" In this professor's department, there was a racial incident involving the graduate students. The suggested response? You guessed it—yet another diversity training. "The response from the diversity inclusion people was like 'Well, we can do a diversity workshop?' Like, what? I could have told you these things don't work back in 2005. It's 2020, right? Why are we going back to these old things that we know don't work? This is just, this is old news."

Another professor expressed a similar frustration over the lack of change: "I'm so sick and tired of diversity training. And just the same old vanilla conversation that happens, it's just like we talked about it, but nothing changes." Across organization types, almost every one of these entry-level professionals had seen at least one diversity training come and go. Not one indicated wholesale improvement in their work environment as a result.

Resource Practices

Resource practices are those identity-conscious practices that focus on getting marginalized employees what they need to succeed. Among these, mentoring was incredibly important across the board. In each organization type and racial group, the benefits of mentors came up frequently and unprompted. The employees I spoke with would mention, "I had to talk to my mentors" when in a difficult situation, or "I wouldn't still be here, but I had very supportive mentors." Mentoring is lauded for good reason; it is one of the diversity initiatives effective at increasing representation in nearly every group studied here.[12]

Employees found mentors in various ways. Some extolled peer mentors who were in the same stage of career and could share strategies. One of those was a Black employee in finance who was in a group chat with three peers in similar companies and positions. He raved, "We always encourage each other and mentor each other. We started out at the same levels; we've been accomplishing all these things together, whether it's increasing our knowledge base, getting certified, higher levels of recognition. That's where I get my mentorship." Others found mentors from past positions or previous schools. Still others found mentors outside of their fields altogether. One pastor spoke of his mentorship by a professor who helped him to understand the racial and cultural dynamics of his role in a diverse church. As the pastor shared, "When I'm really struggling, his theology, his teaching really helps me stay in tune with how I respond."

Although mentorship was extremely important, employees questioned the helpfulness of official mentoring relationships. Many saw it as just another work commitment. Others were concerned that they could not trust the advice of the mentors. One Black assistant professor working in a Northeastern city contrasted the helpfulness of his official mentors with his unofficial ones. "Having to meet with my official mentors, you know, twice a semester, in theory, is a great idea. But sometimes I'm just like, am I actually going to derive value from this meeting? Or would I actually derive more value just from being in my office and working? So, for me personally, I have enough support." Because this professor has built informal networks that were meeting his mentoring need, the assignment of official mentors by the department and the college became more of a chore.

A Black corporate employee expressed the same sentiment when he was offered a mentoring program in the face of his anger over mistreatment within the company. When I asked if he signed up for the program proffered, he replied, "No, I did not sign up for it. The older Black guys on my team, I consider them as my mentors. I go to them, and I'm just like, how do I deal with this? What would you do? I don't want to go through an official program and get locked into something more like a homework assignment than an actual relationship." Neither of these employees denied the power of mentorship. They both actively sought it out. But neither was sold on the official programs that were designed to help them get mentorship. These programs felt more like extra work than extra help to these employees.

Not having the time for official mentoring can lead to the failure of these relationships. A Latino assistant professor was part of a mentoring program for first-year faculty. He explained why this effort quickly folded. The group had trouble coordinating its meetings and eventually stopped trying. "My group just wasn't successful for all sorts of reasons. That was just the luck of the draw; they just didn't get good faculty mentors." Rather than being disappointed, this professor was relieved. Participating in an official mentoring program was not his top priority. "I've just been too busy this first year. I just didn't have the time to even avail myself of these resources."

While official mentoring programs did not provide the employees in this study what they needed, that does not mean that workplaces should end mentoring efforts altogether. If employees of color are left to their own devices in finding mentors, racial gaps in knowledge are reinforced. One Midwestern assistant professor found that to be true when she relied primarily on Black faculty to provide her with mentorship. This opened gaps in her knowledge that she still feels as an assistant professor.

As a graduate student, I felt marginalized very quickly and out of place very quickly and felt like one of the first lessons that I learned as a graduate student was that this is a white space, and I don't belong. And if I'm going to survive, I need to find the people of color that are going to understand the struggle and help me through it. And I did that. But in so doing, there were a set of skills I didn't learn because the other faculty of color didn't seem to have those skills to pass down to me. So, creating dynamic social networks, I never got that skill. Being a part of the communities of scholars, whether that was in a social networking or just like a cross-pollinating capacity, didn't get that skill. Working with others to publish articles, I didn't get that skill. The mentorship that I got was trash because the professors of color were totally overburdened. Had a million students and didn't really know how to develop us professionally. Didn't really know how to teach us how to write. Because my mentors, basically, didn't have a clue what was going on.

As an assistant professor, this employee discovered things others seemed to know about publishing and networks that she never learned from or observed in her mentors. Interestingly, out of her felt deficit, this assistant professor also took on many students to mentor simply because students of color were clamoring for her support. This may have perpetuated the very racial knowledge gaps she was suffering.

Mentoring was viewed as positive and necessary by all employees, but formal mentoring programs were not. The time taken away by formal mentoring was experienced almost as another minority tax, skimming time for more productive activities. The hands-off approach to mentoring also had shortcomings, preventing necessary information from reaching employees of color. However, while letting people find their own mentors can result in information gaps, those gaps are also not solved if formal mentors are not trusted or utilized. To be effective, mentoring should be employee driven but employer supported.

Ethnic affinity groups are another commonplace resource practice. Corporations, churches, and universities often set up spaces where members of particular racial/ethnic groups could gather together for camaraderie and mutual support. Case in point, I am writing these words from the African American Cultural Resource Center at the University of Cincinnati, surrounded by students and faculty who are spread out in a common room, taking a respite from the day. The positive benefit of these spaces is in shrinking the size of an organization, allowing constituencies of color to make friendly connections they may not otherwise make. One employee described how networking within the Black-specific ethnic affinity group helped her secure a new role within the company. "When I got this position, one of the ladies that I did speak with is from the

Employee Resource Group." She further praised the group for how it allowed her to fit in. "I believe that when you're in places like this, you have to have something that is so true towards the African American community because if you don't, you can get lost."

While the networking aspect of this employee resource group yielded positive results, that was not the only purpose of the group. As I asked what other activities occurred in the ethnic affinity group, I found that fully one-third of the group's energy is invested in putting on events so all employees can experience Black culture. "They make sure we do a big Black History Month celebration so that people can come. We have a big auditorium where people could come in and see different types of dance—African dance. We have people who come to do poetry and singing. We try to enlighten people about the culture; we may have a soul food day in the cafeteria."

Special food days in the cafeteria were not unique to this ethnic affinity group. At another company, during a particularly tone-deaf celebration of Black history through food, one Black employee told me disgustedly, "The first thing they said when we walked through this room was, 'Please. Would you like some collard greens and some watermelon?'" This employee, who had protested that the planned celebration "might not go over well," responded with appropriate anger, as did some of his colleagues. "Are you freaking serious? You want me to sit here, have a forum led by the Black people and the minorities in the company who are in these higher positions while you just told us in our face, hey, we are going to do the biggest stereotype, but we value you. There were people who got up and walked out. It was just really bad."

Diversity as commodity requires having something to consume. In some cases, the culture of employees of color via food or music was what was on offer. This happened on "ethnic" days in workplaces. Another example occurred when the Latino/a group of a diverse church was asked to make and serve lunch for the entire church, without the reciprocity of them being served. Whatever the case, when employees of color gathered for their mutual belonging and comfort, an additional task was tacked on to their mission as a group. This was representing their culture for the consumption of others. At the very least, this took away from time they could have spent on tasks relevant to their work. Moreover, it was dehumanizing as they were asked to put a shallow caricature of their culture on display.

Ethnic affinity groups provide networking for employees of color in ways that can be extremely helpful. However, the helpfulness is suboptimized when these same groups are relied upon to present their culture to the rest of the organization or when employees of color undertake tremendous burdens to support them. By keeping these groups as a resource to employees of color, rather than a drain on their capacity, the stated intent of these groups can be more fully realized.

The final resource program described by employees of color was the provision of finances. In most cases, this direct aid was viewed extremely positively. One Latino professor from the Midwest received extra funding for his work. He credited the importance of his ethnic studies department to the university's diversity displays for this gift. "Yeah, I think everywhere ethnic studies programs and initiatives are in decline, and here, not so much. I think if it were made clear that something was being rubbed out, it would hurt diversity marketing. They don't want any news stories in that regard." Because this particular university needed ethnic studies as part of its diversity marketing, the program was well supported, and this professor received funds to help him to execute his research. "They are giving me a buyout of two courses for a quarter and a hundred hours of research assistants. They're paying for students to work for me. And that's great. Like, I don't know that I would have gotten that somewhere else." By having the funding and time to execute research, this professor was able to make faster progress toward his tenure requirements.

In order to be effective, financial support must be sufficient to propel the employee toward their goals. In the above case, because research assistance came with a reduction in the courses, the professor had both resources and enough time to use them. When this does not happen, and insufficient resources are made available to employees, it can again threaten the legitimacy of the employer. Insufficient resources make the recipient question intent. One example of this was communicated by an auto company employee. Their company launched an initiative to help employees of color own their own dealerships. The employee describing the program saw it as little more than window dressing because the program did not address the full structural barriers to owning a dealership. The auto business is full of family legacies that can provide the sons and daughters of auto dealers a significant advantage. There was no recognition of this in the funds provided to potential owners of color. "The auto industry, for lack of better terms, it's a 'good old boy' industry. Like, the owners are lineage. It's 'my dad owned this dealership, his dad owned a dealership, and it's been passed down to me.' And if somebody new wants to enter the ballgame, you have to build brand new. It's a lot of startup costs."

The auto company's effort to provide tangible resources was undermined because what it provided would not allow an employee of color to be successful. Rather than provide confidence to employees of color, this lackluster support simply proves to these employees that their company does not truly understand the barriers they face. "I don't say this to demean it, but I swear it seems like the flavor of the month or year has been diversity and inclusion. They want you to own these dealerships. Hey, we want you to be the face of a dealership, but they don't offer the complete support. They're not providing that real support that you're going to need." Without enough support, employees rightfully wonder who the true beneficiary of this initiative is. When giving financial resources is more about commodification and getting a new face of diversity, these efforts may ultimately fail.

Accountability Practices

Finally, accountability practices hold leadership accountable for meeting diversity goals. This can be done via tying compensation or performance reviews to meeting diversity goals or by hiring a chief diversity officer whose job it is to have the company meet these goals. Accountability practices will often occur in concert with nondiscrimination and resource practices; accountability is focused on the end rather than the means.

The accountability practice that was most evident to employees of color was the presence of a chief diversity officer. For the most part, employees of color felt diversity officers were distant from their everyday needs and not terribly effective at making a difference. One Asian American professor expressed that a diversity office was not of much use to him. He felt that any communication with such an office would invite repercussions. "You don't want to make noise. Like you don't want to be making a stink and going to your dean saying, 'We need to bring the diversity officer and to watch our [job] search for us.' That's not going to look good." The presence of the diversity office does not make a difference in departmental processes such as searches for new faculty if they are not seen as accessible or if asking them in would invite unwarranted attention.

A Black assistant professor had the same skepticism about the proximity of the diversity office to her daily concerns. "One criticism I've had of our chief diversity officer is that he's never once gotten all Black people in the room, or, you know, all marginalized faculty, staff. Call a town hall or something like that, to just ask us, What are the needs of students? What are your needs? How can we serve them?" This question is particularly important at her university—the percentage of faculty of color lags students of color by nearly 20 percent, creating stress for faculty of color in terms of student support. Like many universities, most diversity activities are student-facing with limited programming for faculty and staff. This disconnection was echoed in other universities. One Latina professor had an even stronger critique of the diversity office: "People are getting paid for I don't know what, and that bothers me because they don't even show up to the things we need them to show up to. So, what's the point of them?"

In addition to their concerns about the effectiveness about the diversity office, corporate employees lamented that diversity officer seemed to be the highest position that they could aspire to within their company. As one Black, East Coast account manager commented, "I'm not trying to discredit that, but we are more than just diversity topics. I mean, the head of diversity and inclusion is an amazing position but it's like, we can do more than being chief or head of diversity inclusion, we can do more." That the person in charge of diversity was the most visible Black employee within his company implied that Black employees brought value in the realm of diversity, but not in more central business functions.

Diversity officers as an accountability practice show effectiveness at increasing the representation of employees of color.[13] The drawback to such officers is that they may be more focused on meeting a representation goal than on improving the diversity climate for employees of color. The observations of employees of color bear this out. While they know such offices and officers exist, offices of diversity often feel distant from employees' everyday concerns and work requirements. By and large, the impact of diversity officers' work is either unapparent to, or ineffective for, rank-and-file employees of color.

Changing the Metrics

The implementation of diversity initiatives continues to ignore evidence-based strategies in favor of popular solutions.[14] There is overwhelming evidence for which of these initiatives support the representation of employees of color while avoiding backlash from nontargets.[15] Yet, the most effective programs are seldom put in place. Critics of diversity initiatives have noted that the mismatch between evidence and action is purposeful, arguing that diversity initiatives are not designed to produce racial equality.[16] Employees of color are not oblivious to the shortcomings of diversity initiatives; these programs make employees of color no more likely to believe they will experience equity and belonging within their workplaces.[17]

So how could these initiatives move from diversity displays to vehicles for equity? Simple tweaks could focus workplace initiatives on the success of employees of color without expending significantly more resources. For instance, what if instead of assigning mentors, mentoring initiatives provided employees of color guidance to help them find appropriate mentors, the resources to fund meetings with these mentors, and the management accountability to make sure employees were in active relationship with mentors? Perhaps then organizations could promote mentorship without subjecting employees of color to unhelpful work requirements via assigned mentors. Another simple fix exists when it comes to ethnic affinity groups. Simply remove the burden of cultural celebrations for the masses to ensure that 100 percent of the activities of these groups attend to the employees they purport to serve. Finally, before targeted funding is provided to people of color, workplaces should investigate employees' holistic needs so that funding is sufficient to the challenges that they face. Providing ample funding to fewer participants may be better than inadequate resources for a broader group.

Most of all, any initiatives put in place should be data driven. It is telling that in the fourteen years I was engaged in diversity efforts at an extremely data-driven company, not once did a study about what was effective for employees of color inform our efforts. I had no idea such data existed until I moved from the practice to the study of diversity. Data was one of the most pervasive requests of employees I spoke with. As one Asian American corporate recruiter put it, "KPIs (Key Performance Indicators) are a big thing, but we're not very good at that. So, metrics are needed." Likewise, a Black hospital system employee wants "to have a strategic plan with objectives and tactics. It would be something that would go very deep in terms of strategy and engagement." A Latino assistant professor echoed this sentiment from his liberal arts college: "I've been at three academic institutions now, and I feel like there's a lot of rhetoric. There are always websites on inclusion and diversity. There are committees. But I feel like there's not as much relying on data. Where we are putting our efforts needs to be driven by data." He concluded by saying that to improve the climate for faculty of color, "I would definitely try to make it a little more outcome-driven as opposed to the more political the way it is now." Relying on data combats one of the effects of commodification—threatened legitimacy. When workplaces engage in programs that are effective for employees of color, and share information about that effectiveness, employees become convinced that their organization is committed to their success.

Not just measurement, but measuring the right things is critical here. The targets of diversity initiatives are not only underrepresented, they also experience less pay and fewer promotions than nontargets, exclusion from coworkers, and low status in everyday interactions.[18] The data that racial equity initiatives collect in organizations should delve into each of these areas; just measuring representation is not enough. For smaller organizations, holistic measures could include pay equity audits and 360-degree feedback to leadership on how employees are feeling. Larger organizations can conduct holistic diversity climate surveys, among other measures. With any of these approaches, measurable progress that employees of color see and feel is key to restoring organizational legitimacy.

To create more equitable workplaces, diversity initiatives must be transformed into equity work that is effective for targets and nontargets alike. Initiatives based on data can be effective; the problem is that today so few are data based. In the absence of this careful effort, diversity initiatives will perpetuate the sort of inequality most people think they combat.

8 Dreaming Bigger

Toward Workplace Equity

In arguments for *Students for Fair Admissions v. University of North Carolina (UNC)*, one of two cases that have now overturned the use of racial demographics as a factor in college admissions, Justice Clarence Thomas declared, "I've heard the word diversity quite a few times and I don't have a clue what it means." The lawyer for UNC, Ryan Park, responded with a definition of diversity and a recitation of the educational benefits thereof including "reduced bias" and "more creative thinking and exchange of ideas." Thomas remained unmoved, denying that these were benefits to education. He claimed, parents "send them there [to UNC] to learn physics or chemistry or whatever they're studying." Such a dim view of human variation and the benefits of interaction across different perspectives is clearly unfounded and dangerous. The colorblindness advocated by the US Supreme Court in the decision for this case cannot create a level playing field; it highlights how legal structures normalize, justify, and entrench current racial hierarchies.[1]

Given challenges like this playing out on a national stage, it feels risky to expose the negatives of diversity as I have done in this book. I am wary of my words being used by conservative critics of diversity to fight for a world in which racial disparities are ignored. However, Thomas's attack on diversity also reveals a key reason why this contested territory may not be worth defending. In a very real way, diversity policies are just a compromise that held from the time Justice Powell used it to maintain race-conscious admissions in *Regents of the University of California v. Bakke* until recently. Decisions from the US Supreme Court, the removal of DEI personnel from workplaces, and the jettisoning of diversity statements at universities show that this concession is nearing its end in many areas of life and work.[2] If that is the case, why not move beyond middle ground? Why not instead recognize that racial disparities have continued, somewhat unabated, under diversity policies? Why not fight for the recognition of inequality erased by Justice Powell's opinion? As Justice Harry A. Blackmun concluded in the *Bakke* case, "In order to get beyond racism, we must first take account of race. There is no other way. And in order to treat some persons equally, we must treat them differently."

As reluctant supporters of diversity are abandoning it in favor of colorblindness, so may ardent advocates abandon it but in favor of equity. Recall that equity means everyone has what they need to succeed because there is "fairness in processes, practices, and outcomes within the context of historical, economic, social, and institutional forces that have resulted in an unequal playing field."[3] Dreaming bigger means pushing for equity to become the guiding imperative for initiatives around race in organizations.

The mainstream meanings of diversity revealed in diversity ideology create negative consequences by bringing people of color into majority white spaces for the benefit of white people. These benefits include economic gain, in the form of improved outreach to customers; reputational gain, by being insulated from charges of racism; and cultural gains, through exposure to people from all walks of life. Those benefits are not equally shared by people of color, who become the objects of diversity.

This concluding chapter reviews the evidence I have presented to show how diversity ideology perpetuates racial inequality in the workplace and suggests a new way forward. Workplace racial inequality is not abstract, but can be seen in the bodies, careers, and lives of employees of color. Employees of color point to commodification, a key feature of diversity ideology, as complicit in their negative work experiences. The effects of commodification are distinct from other forms of racial discrimination. Commodification significantly decreases job quality for employees of color through heavy work demands, threatened legitimacy, and subjugated identity, each of which creates the conditions for job strain and its resultant physical and emotional symptoms of stress. As long as commodification remains essential to the systems of meaning attached to diversity, diversity can never lead to racial equity.

It is not just the systems of meaning that white people and institutions attach to diversity, such as commodification, that cause harm. Employees of color also hold a diversity ideology that perpetuates the current state. I have identified the tenets of that ideology as *diversity as philanthropy, diversity as opportunity*, and *diversity as resource*. Through diversity as philanthropy, employees of color hold a shared logic that diversity is about their support for other constituencies of color. Believing that this support is what they are in diverse organizations to provide, they remain in organizations that do not serve them. Diversity as opportunity and diversity as resource represent the ideas that employees of color hold toward the need of white people and organizations for diversity. The former accepts this need as a way to get a foot in the door and the latter uses this need as a way to gain from racial identity. These three tenets perpetuate the dominant diversity ideology by giving employees of color reason to join diverse organizations, submitting to commodification and racial equity labor for the benefit of constituencies of color and the opportunity for personal gain. Because of the efforts of employees of color, organizations are able to continue racial outsourcing, offloading onto employees of color the support of diversity imperatives.[4]

In addition to these ideological supports, there are also structural disparities that uphold current conceptions of diversity. Diverse organizations are racialized as white. This gives them a higher status than majority-minority organizations and confers on them the monetary rewards that come along with high status. Because of both the financial rewards and status they carry, diverse organizations have an advantage in attracting employees of color, such that they can seem like the only choice. This despite the proven benefits of majority-minority organizations, such as HBCUs. To further attract employees of color, diverse organizations may put in place programs such as mentoring, diversity training, and diversity offices. However, when these programs are based on benefits to the organizations rather than the employee, they generate negative backlash from nontargets of diversity efforts that further harms employees of color. In sum, employees of color have paid a steep price because of diversity ideology and the structures that support it. This extraction of value cannot continue if we hope to achieve equitable workplaces.

Equity Ideology vs. Diversity Ideology

Diversity ideology is not the only racial ideology available to individuals and organizations as they determine how to operate. As mentioned, an alternative path is to focus on equity. Contrasting equity to diversity in the context of organizations, sociologists Laura T. Hamilton, Kelly Nielsen, and Veronica Lerma contend that equity logics hail from Civil Rights Era reforms and focus on "addressing race as a system of oppression."[5] Instead of holding representation as a goal, equity logics focus on the erasure of racial disparities.[6] This focus relieves pressure on employees of color by involving all in organizational equity efforts. Equity will require different structures that better "distribute power, resources, and opportunity" in the workplace.[7] Such changes will require an employee-focused reimagining of the workplace as it currently exists.

Let's consider what replacing diversity ideology with equity might mean for some of the employees we have met in this work. Dr. Flint is the assistant professor whose face showed up in a diversity presentation without her permission. In an equity-focused university, there would be no need for these diversity displays to peer institutions. Instead, resources would be focused on ensuring Flint received adequate funding to reverse the disadvantages faculty of color experience in receiving grants for their research, credit for the disproportionate time faculty of color spend mentoring students of color, and flexible teaching evaluations that take into account how students downgrade women of color's knowledge and authority in the classroom.[8] Flint's success rather than reputational advantage would be the key metric.

For Pastor Chu, the counseling pastor who spent most of his time planning and sitting in services, the work burden of having to show his face at the right places and times would be taken away. Chu's responsibilities in the organization would align with his job description rather than the diversity needs of the church. Chu would be valued in the organization for his professional expertise rather than his racial identity. Chu could choose to bring his life experience and perspective to bear when and where he thought appropriate, instead of being the voice for every Asian American.

Tea Lacaba, the marketing professional who had to tag along on trips to show diversity, would have robust social support in her workplace. Because everyone would be invested in making sure her workplace was equitable, she would not experience racial outsourcing that made the needs of Black manufacturing workers her responsibility. The images, trips, and sales calls that Lacaba takes part in would reflect the teams she actually works with. If her company advances, it would be because of what is happening within the company, not the image they put forth. The company and Lacaba would jointly benefit.

At this writing, none of the above scenarios have materialized. In fact, not one of these three employees has remained in their workplace. Flint has moved on to another university position. Chu has left vocational ministry altogether, disaffected with the institution of church as he has seen it. Lacaba has become an entrepreneur after one too many companies used her race as a resource.

While their transitions do not represent the primary path for employees of color in this study, they may be the vanguard of a growing trend. With the murder of George Floyd and subsequent protests in the summer of 2020, workplace dissatisfaction grew.[9] Some Black employees had to take breaks from their workplaces. One said, "I literally just took the week off; I had nothing planned. I just needed a week to decompress." Others have selectively disengaged from work by not talking to coworkers. "I don't really talk on those [Zoom] calls unless somebody asks me to speak. Because again, you know, it's a go in, get my work done, not here to joke around with none of you, log off at this point." With COVID-19 precautions, employees experienced the freedom of remote work, and many remain reticent to return to the office. Their dissatisfaction signals that there may be even more employment transitions to come.

Mind Your Language

How might organizations move into a preferred future focused on equity rather than diversity? One starting point is dispensing with the language of diversity in institutional discourse in favor of equity and ultimately racial justice. This is easier said than done. There are legal, financial, and reputational risks to doing away with a term that is generally viewed positively by the public.[10] In addition, the language of diversity is so entrenched in organizational discourse, it can be difficult to imagine alternatives.

Learning the language of justice for racial matters will require looking outside of white normative organizational models. Here is a place where HBCUs might be instructive. Some of these colleges and universities, instead of promoting diversity as a core value, have values that reflect equity instead. Winston-Salem State is one. They clarify this value by stating the university "believes in a deep individual and institutional responsibility to creatively respond to injustice and work toward the establishment of just, equitable, and sustainable cultural, economic, political and social principles and practices that affirm the worth, value, and dignity of all people." Tuskegee University, using a similar sentiment, has made "Equity, Human Dignity, and Service" its first value.[11] These HBCUs demonstrate that celebrating human diversity is not the end goal, but rather ensuring that the potential of each person is respected.

Although many still say "I don't see race," that statement is increasingly viewed as a sort of blindness that obscures reality. Maybe promoting diversity should become just as much of an anathema. Replacing diversity with the language of equity could restore the moral imperative toward repairing past harms that was stripped from diversity initiatives through the 1980s.[12] Today, most Americans desire demographic diversity, yet they simultaneously reject racial remedies to fix the reasons why all racial groups are not equally represented in the first place.[13] Equity language that specifically addresses racism would render this contradiction nonsensical.

Policy Change

Language without action, though, is seen as "lip service" by employees of color. Take, for example, companies that put out anti-racism statements after George Floyd's murder, which recycled diversity language yet failed to acknowledge companies' complicity in racial violence.[14] Even in workplaces where employees are relatively satisfied, they desire policy and action. As one Asian American recruiter told me, "Responsive love and care has been very immediate. We don't pause when it comes to showing how much we love people and how much we care about them. I think what's more important is, What kind of policies are we going to put into place? What kind of actions are we going to put in? You have to have policy."

As implied in the examples of Flint, Chu, and Lacaba above, effective equity policy is employee focused. It is by examining the real disadvantages that employees of color face and putting in place policies to correct those disadvantages that workplaces become more equitable. By this measure, policy is good when employees of color say it is good in their assessments of workplace climate, opportunities for advancement, and job satisfaction.

Each of the three outcomes of commodification—heavy work burdens, threatened legitimacy, and subjugated identity—can be greatly reduced by policy changes. To lighten heavy work burdens, matching job responsibilities to efforts is critical. Employees should be tasked with what is in their job description and paid appropriately. Where diversity as philanthropy is likely, this means decreasing other responsibilities so that employees of color can be paid and promoted for supporting constituencies of color. This also means an end to racial outsourcing. If organizations want to serve a diverse constituency, they must pay for the support of those students, customers, and congregants, rather than allowing their employees of color to volunteer effort. Finally, equitable workplaces are driven by a belief that talent is distributed equally so advancement should be as well. Today, when candidates of color are disproportionately deemed not ready for promotion, their lack of preparation is assumed as a fact and a personal failure, allowing senior positions to remain disproportionately white. In an equitable organization, the questions turn to supervisors, coworkers, and the balance of the organization, asking, "why haven't we prepared everyone at a proportionate rate?" and "what barriers are in the way?" so that all have a chance to succeed.

To end threatened legitimacy, organizations can refocus on internal rather than external legitimacy. This means efforts toward equity are done without press releases. Organizations would also take on efforts to reduce backlash around the hiring of candidates of color, including promoting a pervasive understanding of structural racial inequality and its effects on processes leading up to hiring.

Subjugated identity would diminish if displaying diversity became less important to companies. No longer needing to commodify the racial identity of their employees would better enable employees to be themselves, because there is no image of non-whiteness to sell. Reducing subjugated identity would also mean a reimagining of what the word "professional" means. Standards of dress, speech, and comportment would be about effectiveness instead of being a proxy for whiteness and/or maleness.

Focusing on the needs of employees will still benefit organizations, but in a different way than diversity displays. Advocates of demographic diversity often recognize the creativity, enhanced decision making, and improved performance that teams made up of people from different backgrounds garner.[15] What these proponents often neglect is that these benefits are moderated by the climate in which demographic diversity occurs.[16] In other words, when you bring people from different racial groups together but fail to listen to each person equally, much of the value of demographic diversity is lost. If workplaces understand and communicate that diversity without equity is of little effect, this message may pave the way for change with employees and their managers.

A focus on equity will also lower attrition. The Great Resignation of 2021 saw workers of all races quitting their jobs in unprecedented numbers. But data from Revelio Labs, an aggregator and standardizer of human resources information, showed that attrition did not hit every company equally.[17] Employees were ten times more likely to leave over corporate culture, including inattention to equity, unethical behavior, and disrespect of employees, than they were over other issues such as compensation. Hearing the needs of employees of color and implementing policies in line with those needs may boost key indicators of corporate culture, such as mutual respect. This behavior can also reduce backlash concerning nondiscrimination measures by reinforcing perceptions of an ethical work climate.[18] As a result, employee-centeredness will help not only employees of color but all employees and will reduce workplace turnover costs.

A Better Story

We know that equitable workplaces are possible because some employees are already experiencing them. Pastor Abagail Brunson is associate pastor at a Midwestern church. She is among the small minority of pastors, professors, and corporate professionals working for healthy diverse organizations. At her church, she is known for her fierce theological intelligence. Pastor Brunson is the only Black pastor on her church staff, but she does not have the heavy work burden of being responsible for all things racial. In fact, her white lead pastor has become a lightning rod for his open and principled stands on racial justice; he takes on this duty partially so that Brunson never has to. She explained, "We're explicit about talking about things that need to be talked about from the pulpit. My pastor is a white man, so he can get away with much more than I can. I know that that's rare, particularly in a multiracial church." Brunson herself has studied diverse churches, so she is not simply idealizing her current situation. Agreeing with the harm many of these churches have caused, she reasoned, "This is part of the work that I'm doing in my own dissertation. There are some multiracial churches that I would not recommend people of color go to. They're harmful and they do more damage than they do good. And they sort of baptize white supremacy and white normativity."

Brunson does not experience threatened legitimacy because her leadership is actively affirmed by her coworkers. So much so that she was offered the position of lead pastor but turned it down so that she could continue pursuing her academic goals alongside her ministry. In the early days of the church, Pastor Brunson did experience being used as a resource for her race. Most notable was the time her former lead pastor asked her and her fiancé (now husband) to attend separate Bible studies so there would be at least one Black person at each! This is not an issue with current leadership. Both Brunson and her position are respected.

The healthy environment Brunson is in has given her perspective as to the appropriate role of pastors of color in diverse churches. She explained, "Black and Latino people in these spaces, too often we play the sacrificial lamb role. When I first started doing this, I genuinely believed that if you just talked enough, you cut your arms and let them watch you bleed enough, then that would be the thing that would solve the problem. I learned that that is not the case." Knowing this, Brunson takes breaks when she needs to. She also works alongside the rest of the staff to make sure Black and Latino/a congregants are not unduly sacrificing their cultural desires for those of whites. "I know that most multiracial churches are white cultured, but we've always said that we should reflect the culture of the community that we're in."

Finally, despite the healthy church she works in, Brunson cultivates majority Black spaces for herself and her family. She and her husband helped found a majority Black school that her children attend. "We have two daughters, and our church is multiracial. They are a part of a lot of different extracurricular activities that are often predominantly white. So, they both go to schools that are Black schools."

Brunson avoids heavy work burdens by spreading the load, threatened legitimacy through the recognition of her leadership, and subjugated identity by rejecting white normativity. These things make Brunson's work more joy than burden. Intentionality, not resources, created this difference, as Brunson's church is smaller than many in this study.

The Equal Part

Noteworthy among Brunson's choices is the balance of diverse and majority-minority spaces for her interactions—something that diversity ideology assumes to be incompatible with racial progress. In his examination of the *Brown v. Board of Education* (1954) decision, legal scholar Derrick Bell traces how integrated came to mean equal. After challenges to the "equal" part of the separate but equal doctrine established by *Plessy v. Fergusson* (1896), law student Pauli Murray came up with a strategy to challenge the "separate" part. Coming at a time when US foreign policy interests were hampered by the illegitimacy of segregated schools, her argument worked, with *Brown v. Board of Education* overturning the legality of segregation in schools. With this decision, however, came the end of efforts toward equal schools. When it was decided that separate is inherently unequal, it was implicitly decided that (legally) integrated is inherently equal. This decision brought negative unintended consequences for Black communities. When *Brown* was enacted, thousands of majority Black schools were closed and Black teachers and administrators were dismissed.[19] What's more, Black students found themselves in environments that were hostile to them, separated them by performance tiers from white students, and were not designed for their advancement.

As the aftermath of *Brown* demonstrates, we must cease conflating integration with equity. This may mean preserving monoethnic spaces as a counterpart to predominantly white ones. This would not advocate for legal segregation, but rather provide support for people of color–led spaces where their needs are centered. It would also mean attention to the ways that diverse organizations may rob resources from these spaces, up to and including reparations from diverse organizations where appropriate. The effort to preserve and fund majority-minority workplaces would occur alongside improvements for employees of color in majority white workplaces.

A Black diversity and inclusion expert I spoke with agreed that this balance is needed on the path forward. Given the challenges employees of color face in diverse spaces, he reasoned that there has to be a credible alternative in the form of majority-minority spaces: "I don't embrace either separation or integration, I'm like, we have to do both. We've got to be doing both. We've got to be very intelligent about how we circulate our children, so they don't get co-opted and assimilated into somebody else's agenda." He recommends entering majority white organizations as "long as you can stay sane," to help those spaces become more equitable. At the same time, building alternatives led by people of color is essential to allow breaks when important for mental health.

One Black pastor I spoke with was even clearer. He wanted to reverse the current movement toward pastors of color working in multiracial churches. "I believe you're better off being the change that you want to see and go out there and start [a church], as opposed to occupying these spaces." Black ministry leaders have encouraged others to leave diverse churches with a social media campaign to #leaveloud by exposing the difficulties that they have faced.[20]

Working for racial justice in some diverse spaces, while strengthening people of color–led ones, could create the right balance among exit, voice, and loyalty.[21] In his book about these three options, economist Albert Hirschman theorizes about the probabilities of giving voice in protest or exiting from an organization when experiencing a decline in benefits. He records that higher barriers to exit organizations increase voice, but I believe strengthening majority-minority organizations as an alternative pathway for employees of color could do the same. When there are credible alternatives to diverse organizations, enough employees of color could exit to create more majority-minority spaces. Simultaneously, enough employees of color would remain in diverse spaces and raise their voices to effect change. This combination, though difficult in light of structural advantages to diverse organizations, could diminish racialized stigma afflicting majority-minority workplaces while improving diverse ones.

Racial Capitalism and Transformational Change

Implementing employee-centered policy and strengthening majority-minority spaces will help lessen commodification. Ultimately, though, economic restructuring is necessary for racially equitable outcomes. In the foundational text *Black Marxism*, Cedric Robinson lays out the case that capitalism and racism grew up together and continue to shape the trajectory of society.[22] All capitalism is racial capitalism to the extent that market activities will inevitably reinforce racial inequity.[23] As such, the only long-term solution is wholesale transformation. This transformation would ensure employees of color benefit from the value they produce and have what they need to succeed. Capitalism has always required the exchange of human lives for money on a value that is determined by race. From the quite literal profit off human bodies in chattel slavery to the profit off the images of employees, there is a straight line of exploitation that informs organizations today. This trade in people has become even more entrenched through neoliberal norms that make every interaction an economic one.[24]

Some employees I spoke with were in agreement that current systems are incapable of producing racial equity. When I asked Dr. Flint what she would do to improve diversity and inclusion on her campus, she felt the only answer was to get rid of it. "I would not call it diversity, equity, and inclusion. I would call it the Reparations Office. There has to be a very real conversation about the history of higher education institutions, its colonial history. So much of its money, why it became a profitable financial institution, is based off of slavery. Even public institutions are deeply entrenched in very racist policies."

An Asian professor agreed that the current strategies, no matter how well executed, would not lead to racial equity. "Not because I say like we're doing everything perfectly, but it feels like we're chipping away at the problem and doing a good job chipping away at it, but not making transformational changes. And there's this desire amongst many of us to make transformational changes." He contended that some operating paradigms would need to be undone for the future to be better than the past.

Arriving at equity also means attending to questions of class privilege. I mention in chapter 1 that this investigation is a classed one because the costs of diversity are costs of the middle class. Creating equitable workplaces for pastors, professors, and professionals alone is not enough; this may do nothing for those people on whom their management-level positions rely. Journalist Eyal Press points out that society's most ethically troubling and taxing work is carried out by low-income workers who are beyond the scope of this investigation.[25] The costs that slaughterhouse employees, correctional officers, oil rig workers, and military drone operators experience from their work also deserve redress. Most of us benefit from their work without critically examining its effects on the people who do this work. Capitalism rests on valuing some people over others; as long as this is true, there can never be equity in work. The present investigation of diversity is meant to be a starting point for challenging commodification, exploitation, and other forms of domination, not an end point.

Dream Bigger

Sociologist Eric Olin Wright, in his work *Real Utopias,* chides social scientists in particular for not acting on the injustices we study: "While we live in a social world that generates harms, we also have the capacity to imagine alternative worlds where such harms are absent."[26] In other words, we do not need to be satisfied with scraps, clinging to the current state of diversity to avoid losing progress. Instead, we can imagine and work toward a world that settles for neither colorblind nor diversity ideologies of race. By being clear-eyed about the entrenched state of racial hierarchy while not abandoning our ideals of the world we desire to see, we can get closer than we are today.

In like manner, the related traditions of Afrofuturism and Africanfuturism can help move us toward transformation.[27] These speculative traditions allow us to imagine a "less constrained Black subjectivity in the future and produce a profound critique of current social, racial, and economic orders."[28] This imagination could be powerful for unmooring taken-for-granted aspects of our current political and economic system, such as accumulation and individualism, without which commodification would be nonsensical. Essential to Afrofuturism and Africanfuturism is a tethering in the current social reality. Starting in the present and extending into visions of the future creates possibilities that are neither childish nor overly optimistic, but worth working toward. As literary scholar S. R. Toliver puts it, "All activism is science fiction, for envisioning a world without oppression requires the active creation of socially just societies formed from innovative ideas and visionary possibilities." Leaning into these traditions may give us the courage to move beyond what seems pragmatic or politically viable. A courage that allows us to actively create a better future than the one we see.

This book intentionally focuses on the experiences of employees of color, believing that understanding their experiences allows us to demand better for workers of all races. There is a growing understanding that focusing on the most marginalized creates gains for everyone.[29] Diversity fails this focus by redistributing organizational power and resources to white people and institutions that already have a surplus of them. On the path to racial equity, then, diversity ideology has been a costly detour. It is time to get back on track.

APPENDIX 1

Study Participants

TABLE 1. Respondent Characteristics

Participant	Profession	Race	Gender	State	Pseudonym
P_1	Pastor	Black	Man	AR	
P_2	Pastor	Black	Man	VA	
P_3	Pastor	Black	Man	NC	
P_4	Pastor	Black	Man	OH	
P_5	Pastor	Black	Man	OH	Bryce Rhodes
P_6	Pastor	Black	Man	NC	Duncan Unger
P_7	Pastor	Black	Man	MO	Brian Clemmons
P_8	Pastor	Black	Man	GA	James Johnson
P_9	Pastor	Black	Man	CA	Darrell Winston
P_10	Pastor	Black	Woman	IL	Abagail Brunson
P_11	Pastor	Latino	Man	AR	
P_12	Pastor	Latina	Woman	CA	Alejandra Castillo
P_13	Pastor	Latino	Man	OH	Jorge Morales
P_14	Pastor	Latino	Man	CA	
P_15	Pastor	Latino	Man	CA	
P_16	Pastor	Asian	Man	OR	
P_17	Pastor	Asian	Man	DC	Alan Wah
P_18	Pastor	Asian	Man	OH	Aaron Chu
P_19	Pastor	Asian	Man	FL	
P_20	Pastor	Asian	Man	TX	
P_21	Pastor	Asian	Woman	OR	
Prof_1	Asst Prof	Black	Woman	OH	
Prof_2	Asst Prof	Black	Woman	OH	

TABLE 1 *(Continued)*

Participant	Profession	Race	Gender	State	Pseudonym
Prof_3	Asst Prof	Black	Woman	NC	Bossie Renner
Prof_4	Asst Prof	Black	Woman	TN	
Prof_5	Asst Prof	Black	Woman	NY	
Prof_6	Asst Prof	Black	Man	NY	
Prof_7	Asst Prof	Black	Man	PA	Sam Johnson
Prof_8	Asst Prof	Black	Woman	CA	Odessa Flint
Prof_9	Asst Prof	Black	Man	OH	August Calvo
Prof_10	Asst Prof	Black	Man	MO	
Prof_11	Asst Prof	Black	Man	DC	
Prof_12	Asst Prof	Latino	Man	CA	
Prof_13	Asst Prof	Latino	Man	OH	
Prof_14	Asst Prof	Latino	Man	IN	
Prof_15	Asst Prof	Latino	Man	OH	Martin Estime
Prof_16	Asst Prof	Latino	Man	IL	
Prof_17	Asst Prof	Latina	Woman	IL	
Prof_18	Asst Prof	Latino	Man	CA	
Prof_19	Asst Prof	Latino	Man	TX	
Prof_20	Asst Prof	Latina	Woman	MN	Evelyn Diaz
Prof_21	Asst Prof	Latina	Woman	VA	
Prof_22	Asst Prof	Asian	Woman	NY	
Prof_23	Asst Prof	Asian	Woman	CA	
Prof_24	Asst Prof	Asian	Woman	TN	
Prof_25	Asst Prof	Asian	Man	FL	
Prof_26	Asst Prof	Asian	Woman	TN	
Emp_1	Recruiter	Black	Woman	OH	Cadence Coaston
Emp_2	PR Manager	Black	Woman	OH	Jamie Bixner
Emp_3	Marketing Manager	Black	Man	OH	
Emp_4	Automotive Finance Manager	Black	Man	NJ	
Emp_5	Wealth Manager	Black	Man	FL	Ayodele Marshall
Emp_6	Project Manager	Black	Woman	DC	

Emp_7	Student Services	Black	Man	OH	
Emp_8	HR Manager	Black	Woman	TX	
Emp_9	Software Engineer	Black	Man	TX	Clayton Hudson
Emp_10	Marketing Manager	Latina	Woman	IL	Tea Lacaba
Emp_11	Radio Personality	Latina	Woman	FL	Carmen Hernández
Emp_12	Engineer	Asian	Woman	MI	
Emp_13	HR Manager	Asian	Woman	TX	

Interview Guide

Employees of Color Interview Guide

Introduction

Thank you for agreeing to participate in this interview. This is a research study. You are here as a result of voluntary participation in this interview addressing your experiences as an employee of color within a diverse organization. This interview will last approximately 90 minutes and will consist of a set of structured questions related to your experiences. To thank you for your participation in the interview, you will receive $20 cash.

The session will be recorded using a digital audio recorder, but only the answers you provide will be recorded. You are not required to answer any of the questions asked and you may exit the interview at any time without penalty. Recordings will be transcribed, and data will be stored on a secure network drive within our office. Recorded sessions will be erased off of the audio devices following transcription. Efforts will be made to keep your study-related information confidential.

During the interview, I may jot a few things down just to remind myself to ask about something later in the interview. I may also need to check the recording device from time to time to make sure it is working, but I am still listening.

Are there any questions before we get started?

Do you consent to participate in the research study?

· · ·

The Organization
1. Tell me a little about the organization you work for.
2. How long have you been working at *(current organization)*?
3. How did you decide to come to *(current organization)*?
4. What were the alternative organizations you considered joining?
5. Can you give me an example of how this organization shows a commitment to racial diversity?
   a. Official mission or vision statement?
   b. Recruiting targets?
   c. Special programs or activities?
6. How did the organization's diversity initiatives factor into your decision to join your current organization?
   a. Part of your decision to stay?
7. How do you racially identify? How do you perceive the racial makeup of your current organization? How about the people you work with on an everyday basis?
   a. Size of organization?

Your Responsibilities
8. What are your primary responsibilities in your current role?
9. Can you describe a time when your racial or ethnic background has been a resource for your organization?
   a. Describe that experience.
   b. What were your feelings related to that experience?
10. Do you participate in any work or committees having to do with diversity?
11. How did you get involved in this type of work?
12. How do your white counterparts participate in this type of work as well?

Diversity Rewards/Challenges/Tensions
13. What does racial diversity mean in your experience?
   a. Do you think your view of diversity aligns with the ways in which your organization thinks about diversity? Why or why not?

14. Would you say that you experience any advantages or benefits as a person of color in an organization committed to diversity? How about any disadvantages or costs?
15. Have you seen times when other groups have experienced these benefits or costs in different ways than your group?

Identity
16. Do you feel like you can be yourself in this organization? (Be ready to specify or elaborate)
17. Do you believe the organization's focus on diversity helps or hinders you in that regard?

Vertical and Horizontal Relationships
18. Can you tell me about your relationship with your supervisor within your current organization?
    a. Do you feel like your perspective and opinions are valued?
       i. Please give an example.
    b. Do you feel like you get the support needed to succeed?
       i. Why or why not?
19. In terms of your relationships with your colleagues, do you think you have integrated well, or would you say you are still finding your way?
    a. Do you feel you have good friendships here?
    b. Are there people here that you could count on if you need support?
       i. Getting work done?
       ii. Emotionally?
       iii. Financially?
       iv. Professional advice and advancement?
    c. Are there any barriers that get in the way of stronger relationships?
20. Ask about people that they supervise.

Ethnic Affinity Environments
21. Are you a part of any voluntary organizations (i.e., churches, civic organization, etc.)?
    a. Are any of these organizations designed for a particular racial group?

    b. If yes, how often does the organization meet?

    c. What kinds of activities does the organization do?

    d. What do you receive from being a member of these organizations?

22. Are you are a member of any groups within this organization designed for a particular racial group (workplace and universities only)?

    a. If yes, how often does the group meet?

    b. What kinds of activities does the group do?

    c. What do you receive from being a member of this group?

Racial Views

23. Do you think your race affects you in your everyday life? Why/why not? Provide an example.

24. Do you think your race affects the experiences you've had in your organization?

    a. Do you think this would change if your organization had different policies regarding diversity?

    b. Can you think of a policy that would improve your experience?

25. Do you think people of color in your organization are treated differently than whites?

26. To what extent do you think policies about racial diversity affect how people think about race?

27. Within your organization's focus on diversity, is there ever any discussion of racial inequality?

    a. If yes, what did you talk about?

    b. How did the organization respond?

    c. If no, why do you think that is?

28. To what extent, if at all, do you believe race matters in America? Why?

Additional Thoughts

29. Is there anything else important about your experience within this organization that you'd like me to know?

Notes

Chapter 1: The Costs of Diversity

1. [Private]. "I just found out that the university president named me by name in an open letter in response to George Floyd's murder as an example of what the university is doing to end racism on campus. My contract hasn't even started, and they've already tried to turn me into a token" *Twitter*, July 13, 2020.

2. E.g., Chang 1999; Emerson 2009; Gurin et al. 2002; Luo and Jamieson-Drake 2009; Roberson and Park 2007.

3. Confessore 2024.

4. Atkinson 2024.

5. This incident aside, I spent four wonderful years at the Maggie Walker Governor's School in Richmond, Virginia. I am grateful for the teachers, administrators, and the brilliant fellow students I journeyed with. The school continues to work on areas of improvement when it comes to racial justice and, responding to the critiques of former students, has recently changed admissions requirements to be more equitable to Latino/a and Black students. See Pauly 2022.

6. E.g., Albritton 2012; Masci 2018.

7. Ishimaru and Galloway 2021: 333. For a helpful discussion contrasting equality with equity, see Brayboy, Castagno, and Maughan 2007. While equality means "sameness of resources and opportunities," equity requires an examination of current and historical disparities as well as the provision of differential resources to correct those disparities.

8. Joyce Bell and Douglas Hartmann's 2007 article "Diversity in Everyday Discourse: The Cultural Ambiguities and Consequences of 'Happy Talk'" reveals just how beloved the term diversity is to the public. This positivity is not shared by scholars, however, who have brought up the negative consequences of diversity, including, for example, Berrey 2015; Dobbin and Kalev 2016; Embrick 2011; Moore and Bell 2011; Warikoo 2016.

9. *Regents of the University of California v. Bakke*, 438 U.S. 265 (1978).

10. E.g., Holland and Ford 2021; Gurin, Nagda, and Lopez 2004; Lipson 2007; Petts and Garza 2021.

11. Edelman 1992.

12. E.g., Edelman 2016; Collins 2011; Kelly and Dobbin 1998.

13. Dougherty, Chaves, and Emerson 2020.

14. Edwards, Christerson, and Emerson 2013.

15. E.g., Quillian et al. 2017; Stainback and Tomaskovic-Devey 2012.

16. Berrey 2015: 5.

17. Hall 1980: 334.

18. Mayorga-Gallo 2019.

19. Mayorga-Gallo 2019: 1789.

20. Estlund 2005: 26.

21. Arciniega 2021.

22. Roberson and Park 2007.

23. Barron and Williams 2017.

24. Warikoo 2016.

25. Ahmed 2007.

26. Herring and Henderson 2012: 629.

27. *Investigations of token status:* Kanter 1977; Christerson and Emerson 2003. *Racialized jobs:* Collins 1997. *Racial discrimination:* Feagin 1991; Lacy 2007. *Managing stigma:* Fleming, Lamont, and Welburn 2012. *Investigation of Blacks navigating white space:* Anderson 2015; Holder, Jackson, and Ponterotto 2015.

28. Wingfield 2019: 167.

29. E.g., Beeman 2022; Dovidio, Gaertner, and Saguy 2015; Smith and Mayorga-Gallo 2017; Embrick 2011; Okuwobi 2019; Oyakaya 2019.

30. Anderson et al. 2022.

31. Berrey 2015: 277.

32. Leong 2013.

33. Cashmore 2002: 327.

34. Ray 2019: 20.

35. Brown and Toyoki 2013.

36. Schoon 2022.

37. E.g., Basu, Dirsmith, and Gupta 1999; MacLean and Behnam 2011; Lee and Yoon 2018.

38. Noy 2008.

39. DeYmaz 2010.

40. E.g., Holland and Ford 2021; Lipson 2007.

41. Berrey 2014.

42. E.g., Ray et al. 2017; Barron 2016; Pippert et al. 2013.

43. Wilson 1987.

44. Reskin 2012.

45. Collins 1997.

46. E.g., Ahmed 2012; Collins 1989; Wingfield 2013.

47. E.g., Allen 1992; Brown and Davis 2001; Fries-Britt and Turner 2002; Minor 2008.

48. Munn 2017.

49. E.g., Cook and Glass 2013; Edwards 2008b.

50. Mayorga-Gallo 2019: 1789.

51. Michael Omi and Howard Winant's *Racial Formation in the United States* defines racial projects as "an effort to organize and distribute resources along particular racial lines" (1994: 125).

Chapter 2: Commodities and Tokens

1. Portions of this chapter were previously printed in *Red Skies: 10 Essential Conversations Exploring Our Future as the Church* (Okuwobi 2022).

2. *Mixed-ish*, "Just the Two of Us," season 2, episode 6, first aired March 2, 2021, show transcript accessed July 21, 2022, https://tvshowtranscripts .ourboard.org/viewtopic.php?f = 677&t = 42927.

3. De Jonge et al., 2000.

4. Akin 2020.

5. Padilla 1994.

6. Segura 2003.

7. Joseph and Hirshfield (2011: 131) propose four aspects of differential legitimacy experienced by faculty of color: "(1) lack of belonging in their department; (2) colleagues questioning their qualifications; (3) colleagues not valuing their research; and (4) faculty of colour feeling the need to prove themselves." All of these aspects carry over into the other diverse workplaces in my sample.

8. Sociologists Donald Tomaskovic-Devey and Dustin Avent-Holt (2019) propose a model of relational inequalities, wherein organizations pool resources that people within those organizations then make claims to. Social closure can exclude members of outgroups from equal access to those resources. Diversity initiatives reinforce that exclusion by making the claims of employees of color seem undeserved and illegitimate.

9. *The Daily Show with Trevor Noah*, season 26, episode 80, first aired April 8, 2021.

10. Basu, Dirsmith, and Gupta (1999), when examining the GAO's auditing processes, found that the work done to appear legitimate to external parties is not distinct from internal processes; rather, the two are deeply intertwined. See also Cole and Salimath 2013; Lee and Yoon 2018.

11. E.g., Bracey and Moore 2017; Ince 2022; Wingfield and Alston 2014.

12. Du Bois 1897.

13. Okuwobi, Montgomery, and Melamed 2023.

14. Melamed et al. 2019.

15. Umaña-Taylor and Shin 2007.

16. Quiroz-Gutierrez 2021.

17. Wells Fargo, Twitter post, June 9, 2021, 10:00 a.m., https://twitter.com /WellsFargo/status/1402626535065014275?s=20&t=4v6-Pfqx7WgQL8z6bpP-ZoQ.

18. In 2020, Wells Fargo paid $7.8 million to settle a hiring discrimination claim. While the company did not admit fault, they agreed to corrective measures to improve hiring practices. During the same year, the bank's CEO blamed a lack of Black employees on the "limited talent pool." The company had previously paid $175 million to settle claims of discrimination against Black and Latino / a borrowers. See Shaban 2020; Smith 2020.

19. Hughey 2012.

20. Okuwobi, Faulk, and Roscigno 2021.

21. Jaschik 2019.

22. E.g., Collins 2011; Meyer and Rowan 1977.

23. Berrey 2015.

24. Roscigno and Yavorsky 2014.

25. Kalev, Dobbin, and Kelly 2006.

26. Ahmed 2007.

27. Collins 1997. For how racialized labor remains widespread, see Abad 2019.

28. E.g., Yoder 1991; Zimmer 1988; Stichman, Hassell, and Archbold 2010; Wingfield 2009.

29. Kanter 1977: 214.

30. Bonilla-Silva 2002.

31. Smith and Mayorga-Gallo 2017; Mayorga-Gallo 2019; Ahmed 2012.

32. Shim 2020.

33. Centeno and Cohen 2012.

34. Thomas 2019; Thomas 2020.

35. Dobbin and Kalev 2022.

36. Harley 2008.

37. Melaku 2019.

38. McMillian Cottom 2015.

39. Yancey and Kim 2008.

40. E.g., Gaddis 2015; Nunley et al. 2015; Pager 2003.

41. Chandola and Zhang 2018.

Chapter 3: One of the Things about Bridges Is They Get Walked On

1. E.g., Burgard and Lin 2013; Ducharme and Martin 2000; Glavin, Schieman, and Reid 2011.

2. Richeson, Trawalter, and Shelton 2005.

3. Edwards 2014.

4. E.g., DeSanto Iennaco et al. 2010; Fan et al. 2019; Nomura et al. 2009; Karasek and Theorell 1990.

5. E.g., Assari and Bazargan 2019; Hurtado et al. 2012.

6. Lawrence 2024.

7. In a metanalysis of Black/white job satisfaction, whites were found to be slightly more satisfied with their work on average. This gap was heightened in

more complex jobs where disadvantages due to race would be heightened. Koh, Shen, and Lee 2016.

8. Wingfield 2019.

9. Brown and Toyoki 2013.

10. This saying comes from Luke 14:28 in the Christian Bible: "For which of you, desiring to build a tower, does not first sit down and count the cost, whether he has enough to complete it?"

11. bell hooks 1992: 42.

12. Okuwobi, Munn, and Edwards 2024.

13. Ecklund 2005.

14. Uwan 2019.

15. Bolger et al. 1989.

16. Rock 2020.

17. Collins 1986.

18. Leong 2013: 2208.

19. Fish 1997.

20. Parasuraman 1982.

21. Cohen and Wills 1985.

22. E.g., Hodson 1996; Judge et al. 2001; Lamont 2000; Spector 1986.

23. Cech 2021.

24. DeCarufel and Schaan 1990: 86.

25. Theologian Richard Niebuhr writes about four distinct aspects of calling to vocational ministry. This statement summarizes personal calling, which he argues should also be confirmed by the gifts one has and the community in which one ministers. Niebuhr 1956: 64.

26. E.g., Clinton, Conway, and Sturges 2016; Pitt 2012.

27. Kalleburg 2011.

28. E.g., Hofhuis, Van der Zee, and Otten 2014; Singh and Selvarajan 2013.

Chapter 4: Honorary Whites and Collective Blacks

1. While all employees interviewed are US-based, not all would identify as Asian American (some being Asian Canadian, for example). Here, I use Asian American when it is accurate to the literature I am citing or to the participant I am describing, but Asian to refer to the sample as a whole.

2. Park 1924.

3. Lee and Sheng 2023.

4. Bonilla-Silva 2004.

5. Lee and Kye 2016.

6. Kiang et al. 2017.

7. Lee and Zhou (2015) find that most of their Chinese and Vietnamese interviewees embraced the model minority myth as a pathway to higher achievement in education and in the workplace. Huang (2020) finds that second-generation Asian American workers believe they are stereotyped positively and even given latitude not provided to other employees of color.

8. Huang 2020.

9. Brown et al. 2022.

10. E.g., Ray et al. 2017; Pippert et al. 2013; Hughey 2012.

11. Flores-Gonzalez 2018.

12. Flores-Gonzalez 2018.

13. Works including *Hood Feminism* (Kendall 2020) highlight the ways that "solidarity" among women has often excluded women of color.

14. Although those of Latino/a or Hispanic ethnicity have often had to choose Black or white as a racial descriptor on official surveys such as the census, Hitlin, Brown, and Elder (2007) find that the majority selecting Hispanic ethnicity view their racial identity as distinct from Black or white. Frank, Akresh, and Lu (2010) find that with greater exposure to the US racial system comes a higher likelihood of identifying as Latino/a or Hispanic rather than white.

15. Lee and Bean 2007.

Chapter 5: "I'm Improving It for Us"

1. Portions of this chapter previously appeared in "Diversity as Philanthropy: Diversity Ideology among Pastors, Professors, and Professionals of Color" (Okuwobi 2024). Permission to reprint the material in this form is acknowledged and appreciated.

2. Mayorga-Gallo 2019.

3. Foucault 2010.

4. Perry 2012.

5. E.g., Gaddis 2015; Nunley et al. 2015.

6. Hamilton, Nielsen, and Lerma 2022: 4.

7. Wingfield 2019: 168.

8. O'Meara et al. 2020.

9. Moore and Blake 2015.

10. Bourdieu 1985.

11. Banks 2012.

12. Goldfarb 2011: 737.

13. E.g., Gomez 2020; Valente and Berry 2017.

14. As with all racial groups, Asian Americans are not monolithic in this sense. However, political scientist Julie Lee Merseth (2020) finds that people who strongly identify as Asian American tend to show a sense of linked fate that extends to other nonwhite groups. This tendency may be enhanced within diverse organizations where racial identity is made hypervisible. See also Edwards and Kim 2019.

15. E.g., Wuthnow 2011; Davidson and Pyle 1994.

16. Bekkers and Wiepking 2011; Feischmidt and Zakariás 2020.

17. E.g., Andreoni, Harbaugh, and Vesterlund 2010; Nagel 1970.

18. Monroe 1994: 862.

19. Du Bois 1903.

20. Banks 2021.

21. Vallejo 2015.

22. Bell 1980.

23. Fahle et al. 2020.

24. Severson 2024.

25. Pfeffer and Salancik 1978.

26. Nienhüser 2008.

27. Munn 2019.

28. Mayorga-Gallo 2014: 149.

29. Tressie McMillan Cottom [@tressiemcphd]: "This place was fucked up when you got here; it will be fucked up when you leave here. All you can control is how much you let it fuck you up in the process." *Twitter,* February 10, 2020.

Chapter 6: Making Diversity the Only Option

1. Ridgeway and Walker 1995.

2. Ray 2019; Wooten and Couloute 2017.

3. Ray 2019.

4. Wooten 2015.

5. Wolfe 2015.

6. Bell and Hartmann 2007.

7. Fields and Fields 2012.

8. Ahmed 2012.

9. Okuwobi, Munn, and Edwards 2024.

10. Damaske 2009.

11. Stinchcombe 1965.

12. E.g., Allen 1992; Brown and Davis 2001; Fries-Britt and Turner 2002; Minor 2008.

13. Colen, Pinchak, and Barnett 2021.

14. Ray 2019.

15. Edwards 2008a.

16. Emerson and Bracey 2024.

17. Haney-Lopez 2006.

18. Collins 1997.

19. Cheney and Ashcraft 2007: 157.

20. Ashcraft et al. 2012.

21. Cassidy and Mikulich 2007.

22. DiMaggio and Powell 1983.

23. Garbes 2021.

24. Thumma and Travis 2007.

25. Patrick 2021.

26. Okuwobi, Munn, and Edwards 2024.

27. Ray 2019.

Chapter 7: Formal Diversity Practices

1. *The Office*, "Diversity Day," season 1, episode 2, first aired March 29, 2005, show transcript accessed August 2, 2022, https://subslikescript.com /series/The_Office-386676/season-1/episode-2-Diversity_Day.

2. If you've not seen it, seriously, check out this clip. It is infinitely cringey: https://www.nbc.com/the-office/video/diversity-day/3839859.

3. Leslie 2019.

4. Jackson, Joshi, and Erhardt 2003.

5. Gonzalez and DeNisi 2009.

6. E.g., Dobbin, Shrage, and Kalev 2015; Leslie 2019.

7. Leslie 2019.

8. E.g., Dobbin and Kalev 2022; Kalev, Dobbin, and Kelly 2006; Kulik and Roberson 2008.

9. Noon 2018.

10. Smith 2020.

11. For a discussion of racialized expertise, see Portocarrero 2023.

12. Dobbin and Kalev 2022.

13. Dobbin and Kalev 2016.

14. Edelman et al. 2011.

15. In their 2022 *Getting to Diversity: What Works and What Doesn't*, sociologists Frank Dobbin and Alexandra Kalev recommend shifting from efforts focused on manager bias to those that democratize career systems, work-life accommodations, and the ability of managers to be change agents. While this excellent book provides newer and more extensive evidence for recommendations on how to improve diversity, it also reinforces the findings these scholars have offered with insufficient uptake from workplaces for over twenty years. See, for example, Kelly and Dobbin 1998; Kalev, Dobbin, and Kelly 2006; Dobbin and Kalev 2016.

16. Moore and Bell 2011.

17. Dover, Kaiser, and Major 2020.

18. E.g., Bertrand and Hallock 2001; Joshi, Son, and Roh 2015; Mor Barak, Cherin, and Berkman 1998.

Chapter 8: Dreaming Bigger

1. Moore 2008.

2. E.g., Crumley 2024; Robinson and Shah 2024.

3. Ishimaru and Galloway 2021: 333.

4. I deal with racial equity labor and racial outsourcing extensively in chapter 4. For a discussion of racial equity labor among university faculty of color, see Hamilton, Nielsen, and Lerma 2022. For a discussion of racial outsourcing, see Wingfield 2019.

5. Hamilton, Nielsen, and Lerma 2022: 4.

6. Jayakumar and Museus 2011.

7. Sobering 2019.

8. E.g., Griffin, Bennett, and Harris 2013; Heffernan 2021; O'Meara et al. 2020; Thomson, Salazar, and Ecklund 2021.

9. A survey by the Slack Future Forum found that 97 percent of Black workers wanted fully remote or hybrid workplaces. This compared to 79 percent of white workers. Black workers also report higher workplace belonging while working from home. See Tulshyan 2021.

10. Bell and Hartmann 2007.

11. For a discussion of HBCUs and diversity, see Okuwobi, Faulk, and Roscigno 2021.

12. Lorbiecki and Jack 2000.

13. Anderson et al. 2022.

14. Mull 2020.

15. For a review, see van Knippenberg and Schippers 2007.

16. Homan et al. 2007.

17. Sull, Sull, and Zweig 2022; Revelio Labs, Culture 500 data.

18. Leslie 2019.

19. Bell 2005.

20. The Witness is a Black Christian Collective that creates articles podcasts and other communications on Black Christian identity. In 2021, they launched a campaign named #Leaveloud to encourage Black Christians to leave multiracial churches where they were being dishonored and to be vocal about why they were leaving. See https://thewitnessbcc.com/ptm-what-is -leaveloud/.

21. Hirschman 1970.

22. Robinson 2000.

23. Melamed 2011.

24. Centeno and Cohen 2012.

25. Press 2021.

26. Wright 2011.

27. The term Afrofuturism was coined in 1993 by Mark Dery in the essay "Black to the Future: Interviews with Samuel R. Delany, Greg Tate, and Tricia Rose." It is a speculative tradition imagining life and technology beyond the racism faced by the African Diaspora. Correcting for Western-centric thinking in Afrofuturism, author Nnedi Okorafor defined Africanfuturism in 2019. Africanfuturism is "a sub-category of science fiction" that is "similar to 'Afrofuturism'" but more deeply "rooted in African culture, history, mythology and

point-of-view as it then branches into the Black diaspora, and it does not privilege or center the West."

28. English and Kim 2013: 217.

29. The "Black Women Best" framework was conceptualized by Janelle Jones, chief economist at the Department of Labor. It posits that if Black women are thriving, then the economy must be working for everyone else. It also claims that by attending to the experiences of Black women, we understand more about how the economy is working for everyone. The framework includes economic relief through guaranteed income, single-payer health care, and increased labor protections. https://rooseveltinstitute.org/wp-content /uploads/2020/09/RI_Black-Women-Best_IssueBrief-202009.pdf.

References

Abad, Melissa V. 2019. "Race, Knowledge, and Tasks: Racialized Occupational Trajectories." In *Race, Organizations, and the Organizing Process*, vol. 60, *Research in the Sociology of Organizations*, edited by Melissa W. Wooten, 111–30. Bingley, UK: Emerald.

Ahmed, Sara. 2007. "'You End Up Doing the Document Rather Than Doing the Doing': Diversity, Race Equality and the Politics of Documentation." *Ethnic & Racial Studies* 30(4): 590–609.

Ahmed, Sara. 2012. *On Being Included: Racism and Diversity in Institutional Life*. Durham, NC: Duke University Press.

Akin, Molly. 2020. "The Time Tax Put on Scientists of Colour." *Nature* 583(1): 479.

Albritton, Travis J. 2012. "Educating Our Own: The Historical Legacy of HBCUs and Their Relevance for Educating a New Generation of Leaders." *Urban Review: Issues and Ideas in Public Education* 44(3): 311–31.

Allen, Walter. 1992. "The Color of Success: African-American College Student Outcomes at Predominantly White and Historically Black Public Colleges and Universities." *Harvard Educational Review* 62: 26–44.

Anderson, Elijah. 2015. "The White Space." *Sociology of Race and Ethnicity* 1(1): 10–21.

Anderson, Nick, Robert Barnes, Scott Clement, and Emily Guskin. 2022. "Over 6 in 10 Americans Favor Leaving Race Out of College Admissions, Post-Schar School Poll Finds." *Washington Post*, October 22. Retrieved November 1, 2022. https://www.washingtonpost.com/education/2022/10/22/race-college-admissions-poll-results/.

Andreoni, James, William T. Harbaugh, and Lise Vesterlund. 2010. "Altruism in Experiments." In *Behavioural and Experimental Economics, The New Palgrave Economics Collection*, edited by S. N. Durlauf and L. E. Blume. 6–13. London: Palgrave Macmillan.

Arciniega, Luzilda. 2021. "Selling Diversity to White Men: How Disentangling Economics from Morality Is a Racial and Gendered Performance." *Organization* 28(2): 228–46.

Ashcraft, Karen Lee, Sara Louise Muhr, Jens Rennstam, and Katie Sullivan. 2012. "Professionalization as a Branding Activity: Occupational Identity and the Dialectic of Inclusivity-Exclusivity." *Gender, Work & Organization* 19(5): 467–88.

Assari, Shervin, and Mohsen Bazargan. 2019. "Unequal Associations between Educational Attainment and Occupational Stress across Racial and Ethnic Groups." *International Journal of Environmental Research and Public Health* 16(19): 3539. doi: 10.3390/ijerph16193539.

Atkinson, Brianna. 2024. "UNC BOG Votes to Eliminate DEI Policy." WUNC, May 23. Retrieved May 29, 2024. https://www.wunc.org/2024-05-23/unc -bog-vote-eliminate-dei-policy.

Banks, Patricia A. 2012. "Cultural Socialization in Black Middle-Class Families." *Cultural Sociology* 6(1): 61–73.

Banks, Patricia A. 2021. "High Culture, Black Culture: Strategic Assimilation and Cultural Steering in Museum Philanthropy." *Journal of Consumer Culture* 21(3): 660–82. doi: 10.1177/1469540519846200.

Barris, Kenya, Tracee Ellis Ross, and Peter Saji (writers); Shiri Appleby (director). 2021. "Just the Two of US." Season 2, episode 6 in *Mixed-ish*, executive producers Anthony Anderson, Tracee Ellis Ross, Brian Dobbins, Helen Sugland, Kenya Barris, Peter Saji, Laurence Fishburne, Randall Winston, Karin Gist, and Courtney Lilly. American Broadcasting Company.

Barron, Jessica M. 2016. "Managed Diversity: Race, Place, and an Urban Church." *Sociology of Religion* 77(1): 18–36.

Barron, Jessica M., and Rhys H. Williams. 2017. *The Urban Church Imagined: Religion, Race, and Authenticity in the City*. New York: NYU Press.

Basu, Onker N., Mark W. Dirsmith, and Parveen P. Gupta. 1999. "The Coupling of the Symbolic and the Technical in an Institutionalized

Context: The Negotiated Order of the GAO's Audit Reporting Process."
American Sociological Review 64(4): 506–26.

Beeman, Angie. 2022. *Liberal White Supremacy: How Progressives Silence Racial and Class Oppression*. Athens: University of Georgia Press.

Bekkers, René, and Pamala Wiepking. 2011. "A Literature Review of Empirical Studies of Philanthropy: Eight Mechanisms That Drive Charitable Giving." *Nonprofit and Voluntary Sector Quarterly* 40(5): 924–73. doi: 10.1177/0899764010380927.

Bell, Derrick A., Jr. 1980. "*Brown v. Board of Education* and the Interest -Convergence Dilemma." *Harvard Law Review* 93(3): 518–34.

Bell, Derrick A., Jr. 2005. "The Unintended Lessons in *Brown v. Board of Education*." *New York School Law Review* 49(4): 1053–67.

Bell, Joyce M., and Douglas Hartmann. 2007. "Diversity in Everyday Discourse: The Cultural Ambiguities and Consequences of 'Happy Talk.'" *American Sociological Review* 72(6): 895–914.

Berrey, Ellen. 2014. "Breaking Glass Ceilings, Ignoring Dirty Floors: The Culture and Class Bias of Diversity Management." *American Behavioral Scientist* 58(2): 347–70. doi: 10.1177/0002764213503333.

Berrey, Ellen C. 2015. *The Enigma of Diversity: The Language of Race and the Limits of Racial Justice*. Chicago: University of Chicago Press.

Bertrand, Marianne, and Kevin F. Hallock. 2001. "The Gender Gap in Top Corporate Jobs." *ILR Review* 55(1): 3–21.

Bolger, Niall, Anita DeLongis, Ronald C. Kessler, and Elaine Wethington. 1989. "The Contagion of Stress across Multiple Roles." *Journal of Marriage and the Family* 51(1): 175–83.

Bonilla-Silva, Eduardo. 2002. "The Linguistics of Color-Blind Racism: How to Talk Nasty about Blacks without Sounding 'Racist.'" *Critical Sociology* 28(1/2): 41–64.

Bonilla-Silva, Eduardo. 2004. "From Bi-Racial to Tri-Racial: Towards a New System of Racial Stratification in the USA." *Ethnic & Racial Studies* 27(6): 931–50. doi: 10.1080/0141987042000268530.

Bourdieu, Pierre. 1985. "The Social Space and the Genesis of Groups." *Theory and Society* 14: 723–44.

Bracey, Glenn E., and Wendy Leo Moore. 2017. "'Race Tests': Racial Boundary Maintenance in White Evangelical Churches." *Sociological Inquiry* 87(2): 282–302. doi: 10.1111/soin.12174.

Brayboy, Bryan McKinley Jones, Angelina E. Castagno, and Emma Maughan. 2007. "Equality and Justice for All? Examining Race in Education Scholarship." *Review of Research in Education* 31(1): 159–94.

Brown, Andrew D., and Sammy Toyoki. 2013. "Identity Work and Legitimacy." *Organization Studies* 34(7): 875–96.

Brown, M. Christopher, and James Earl Davis. 2001. "The Historically Black College as Social Contract, Social Capital, and Social Equalizer." *Peabody Journal of Education* 76(31).

Brown, Tony N., Chase L. Lesane-Brown, Rachell Davis, and Michael A. Carroll. 2022. "Viral Racism via Videos: A Study of Asians' Experiences of Interpersonal Discrimination Because of COVID-19." *Social Currents* 9(5): 486–505. doi: 10.1177/23294965221098973.

Burgard, Sarah A., and Katherine Y. Lin. 2013. "Bad Jobs, Bad Health? How Work and Working Conditions Contribute to Health Disparities." *American Behavioral Scientist* 57(8): 1105–27.

Cashmore, Ellis. 2002. "Behind the Window Dressing: Ethnic Minority Police Perspectives on Cultural Diversity." *Journal of Ethnic and Migration Studies* 28(2): 327–41.

Cassidy, Laurie M., and Alexander Mikulich. 2007. *Interrupting White Privilege: Catholic Theologians Break the Silence*. New York: Orbis Books.

Cech, Erin A. 2021. *The Trouble with Passion: How Searching for Fulfillment at Work Fosters Inequality*. Oakland: University of California Press.

Centeno, Miguel A., and Joseph N. Cohen. 2012. "The Arc of Neoliberalism." *Annual Review of Sociology* 38(1): 317–40.

Chandola, Tarani, and Nan Zhang. 2018 "Re-Employment, Job Quality, Health and Allostatic Load Biomarkers: Prospective Evidence from the UK Household Longitudinal Study." *International Journal of Epidemiology* 47(1): 47–57.

Chang, Mitchell J. 1999. "Does Racial Diversity Matter? The Educational Impact of a Racially Diverse Undergraduate Population." *Journal of College Student Development* 40(1): 377–95.

Cheney, George, and Karen Lee Ashcraft. 2007. "Considering 'the Professional' in Communication Studies: Implications for Theory and Research within and beyond the Boundaries of Organizational Communication." *Communication Theory* 17(2): 146–75.

Christerson, Brad, and Michael Emerson. 2003. "The Costs of Diversity in Religious Organizations: An In-Depth Case Study." *Sociology of Religion* 64(2): 163–81.

Clinton, Michael E., Neil Conway, and Jane Sturges. 2016. " 'It's Tough Hanging-up a Call': The Relationships between Calling and Work Hours, Psychological Detachment, Sleep Quality, and Morning Vigor." *Journal of Occupational Health Psychology* 22(1): 28.

Cohen, Sheldon, and Thomas Wills. 1985. "Stress, Social Support, and the Buffering Hypothesis." *Psychological Bulletin* 98(1): 310–57.

Cole, Brooklyn M., and Manjula S. Salimath. 2013. "Diversity Identity Management: An Organizational Perspective." *Journal of Business Ethics* 116(1): 151–61.

Colen, Cynthia G., Nicolo P. Pinchak, and Kierra S. Barnett. 2021. "Racial Disparities in Health among College Educated African-Americans: Can HBCU Attendance Reduce the Risk of Metabolic Syndrome in Midlife?" *American Journal of Epidemiology* 190(4): 553–61.

Collins, Patricia Hill. 1986. "Learning from the Outsider Within: The Sociological Significance of Black Feminist Thought." *Social Problems* 33(6): 14–32.

Collins, Sharon. 1989. "The Marginalization of Black Executives." *Social Problems* 36(4): 317–31.

Collins, Sharon. 1997. *Black Corporate Executives: The Making and Breaking of a Black Middle Class—Labor and Social Change.* Philadelphia: Temple University Press.

Collins, Sharon. 2011. "Diversity in the Post Affirmative Action Labor Market: A Proxy for Racial Progress?" *Critical Sociology* 37(5): 521–40.

Confessore, Nicholas. 2024. " 'America Is under Attack': Inside the Anti-D.E.I. Crusade." *New York Times*, January 20.

Cook, Alison, and Christy Glass. 2015. "The Power of One or Power in Numbers? Analyzing the Effect of Minority Leaders on Diversity Policy and Practice." *Work and Occupations* 42(2): 183–215.

Crumley, Bruce. 2024. "Diversity Policy Backlash Drives Cuts to DEI Staff." Inc.com. Retrieved June 5, 2024. https://www.inc.com/bruce-crumley /diversity-policy-backlash-drives-cuts-to-dei-staff.html.

Damaske, Sarah. 2009. "Brown Suits Need Not Apply: The Intersection of Race, Gender, and Class in Institutional Network Building." *Sociological Forum* 24(2): 402–24.

Davidson, James D., and Ralph E. Pyle. 1994. "Passing the Plate in Affluent Churches: Why Some Members Give More Than Others." *Review of Religious Research* 36(2): 181–96.

DeCarufel, André, and Jean-Louis Schaan. 1990. "The Impact of Compressed Work Weeks on Police Job Involvement." *Canadian Police College Journal* 14(2): 81–97.

De Jonge, Jan, Hans Bosma, Richard Peter, and Johannes Siegrist. 2000. "Job Strain, Effort-Reward Imbalance and Employee Well-Being: A Large-Scale Cross-Sectional Study." *Social Science & Medicine* 50(9): 1317–27.

Dery, Mark 1994. "Black to the Future: Interviews with Samuel R. Delany, Greg Tate, and Tricia Rose." In *Flame Wars: The Discourse of Cyberculture*, edited by Mark Dery, 179–222. Durham, NC: Duke University Press.

DeSanto Iennaco, Joanne, Mark R. Cullen, Linda Cantley, Martin D. Slade, Martha Fiellin, and Stanislav V. Kasl. 2010. "Effects of Externally Rated Job Demand and Control on Depression Diagnosis Claims in an Industrial Cohort." *American Journal of Epidemiology* 171(3): 303–11.

DeYmaz, Mark. 2010. *Building a Healthy Multi-Ethnic Church: Mandate, Commitments and Practices of a Diverse Congregation.* Hoboken, NJ: John Wiley & Sons.

DiMaggio, Paul, and Walter W. Powell. 1983. "The Iron Cage Revisited: Collective Rationality and Institutional Isomorphism in Organizational Fields." *American Sociological Review* 48(2): 147–60.

Dobbin, Frank, and Alexandra Kalev. 2016. "Why Diversity Programs Fail." *Harvard Business Review* 94(7): 14.

Dobbin, Frank, and Alexandra Kalev. 2022. *Getting to Diversity: What Works and What Doesn't.* Cambridge, MA: Harvard University Press.

Dobbin, Frank, Daniel Schrage, and Alexandra Kalev. 2015. "Rage against the Iron Cage: The Varied Effects of Bureaucratic Personnel Reforms on Diversity." *American Sociological Review* 80(5): 1014–44.

Dougherty, Kevin D., and Kimberly R. Huyser. 2008. "Racially Diverse Congregations: Organizational Identity and the Accommodation of Differences." *Journal for the Scientific Study of Religion* 47(1): 23–44.

Dougherty, Kevin D., Mark Chaves, and Michael O. Emerson. 2020. "Racial Diversity in U.S. Congregations, 1998–2019." *Journal for the Scientific Study of Religion* 59(4): 651–62. doi: 10.1111/jssr.12681.

Dover, Tessa L., Cheryl R. Kaiser, and Brenda Major. 2020. "Mixed Signals: The Unintended Effects of Diversity Initiatives." *Social Issues and Policy Review* 14(1): 152–81.

Dovidio, John F., Samuel L. Gaertner, and Tamar Saguy. 2015. "Color-Blindness and Commonality." *American Behavioral Scientist* 59(11): 1518–38.

Du Bois, W. E. B. 1897. "Strivings of the Negro People." *Atlantic Monthly* 80(8): 194-98. http://www.americasinging.com/wordpress2/wp-content/uploads/2009/11/ WEB-DuBois.pdf.

Du Bois, W. E. B. 1903. *The Talented Tenth*. New York: James Pott.

Ducharme, Lori J., and Jack K. Martin. 2000. "Unrewarding Work, Coworker Support, and Job Satisfaction: A Test of the Buffering Hypothesis." *Work and Occupations* 27(2): 223–43.

Ecklund, Elaine Howard. 2005. " 'Us' and 'Them': The Role of Religion in Mediating and Challenging the 'Model Minority' and Other Civic Boundaries." *Ethnic and Racial Studies* 28(1): 132–50.

Edelman, Lauren B. 1992. "Legal Ambiguity and Symbolic Structures: Organizational Mediation of Civil Rights Law." *American Journal of Sociology* 97(6): 1531–76.

Edelman, Lauren B. 2016. *Working Law*. Chicago: University of Chicago Press.

Edelman, Lauren B., Linda H. Krieger, Scott R. Eliason, Catherine R. Albiston, and Virginia Mellema. 2011. "When Organizations Rule: Judicial Deference to Institutionalized Employment Structures." *American Journal of Sociology* 117(3): 888–954.

Edwards, Korie L. 2008a. "Bring Race to the Center: The Importance of Race in Racially Diverse Religious Organizations." *Journal for the Scientific Study of Religion* 47(1): 5–9.

Edwards, Korie L. 2008b. *The Elusive Dream: The Power of Race in Interracial Churches*. Oxford: Oxford University Press.

Edwards, Korie L. 2014. "Role Strain Theory and Understanding the Role of Head Clergy of Racially Diverse Churches." *Sociology of Religion* 75(1): 57-79.

Edwards, Korie L., Brad Christerson, and Michael O. Emerson. 2013. "Race, Religious Organizations, and Integration." *Annual Review of Sociology* 39(1): 211–28.

Edwards, Korie L., and Rebecca Kim. 2019. "Estranged Pioneers: The Case of African American and Asian American Multiracial Church Pastors." *Sociology of Religion* 80(4): 456–77.

Embrick, David G. 2011. "The Diversity Ideology in the Business World: A New Oppression for a New Age." *Critical Sociology* 37(5): 541–56.

Emerson, Michael O. 2009. "Managing Racial Diversity: A Movement toward Multiracial Congregations." Annual Meeting of the American Sociological Association, San Francisco, CA, August.

Emerson, Michael O., and Glenn E. Bracey II. 2024. *The Religion of Whiteness: How Racism Distorts Christian Faith.* New York: Oxford University Press.

English, Daylanne K., and Alvin Kim. 2013. "Now We Want Our Funk Cut: Janelle Monáe's Neo-Afrofuturism." *American Studies* 52(4): 217–30.

Estlund, Cynthia L. 2005. "Putting Grutter to Work: Diversity, Integration, and Affirmative Action in the Workplace." *Berkeley Journal of Employment & Labor Law* 26(1): 1–39.

Fahle, Erin M., Sean F. Reardon, Kalogrides Demetra, Ericka S. Weathers, and Jang Heewon. 2020. "Racial Segregation and School Poverty in the United States, 1999–2016." *Race and Social Problems* 12(1): 42–56. doi: 10.1007/s12552-019-09277.

Fan, Wen, Phyllis Moen, Erin L. Kelly, Leslie B. Hammer, and Lisa F. Berkman. 2019. "Job Strain, Time Strain, and Well-Being: A Longitudinal, Person-Centered Approach in Two Industries." *Journal of Vocational Behavior* 110: 102–16.

Feagin, Joe R. 1991. "The Continuing Significance of Race: Antiblack Discrimination in Public Places." *American Sociological Review* 56(1): 101–16.

Feischmidt, Margit, and Ildikó Zakariás. 2020. "How Migration Experience Affects the Acceptance and Active Support of Refugees? Philanthropy and Paid Work of Hungarian Migrants in the German Immigrant Service." *Journal of Immigrant & Refugee Studies* 18(4): 481–97. doi: 10.1080/15562948.2020.1724353.

Fields, Karen, and Barbara Fields. 2012. *Racecraft.* London: Verso.

Fish, Stanley 1997. "Boutique Multiculturalism, or Why Liberals Are Incapable of Thinking about Hate Speech." *Critical Inquiry* 23(2): 378.

Fleming, Crystal M., Michèle Lamont, and Jessica S. Welburn. 2012. "African Americans Respond to Stigmatization: The Meanings and Salience of Confronting, Deflecting Conflict, Educating the Ignorant and 'Managing the Self.'" *Ethnic and Racial Studies* 35(3): 400–417.

Flores-González, Nilda. 2018. *Citizens but Not Americans: Race and Belonging among Latino Millennials*. New York: NYU Press.

Foucault, Michel. 2010. *The Government of Self and Others: Lectures at the Collège de France 1982–1983*. Edited by Frédéric Gros. Springer.

Frank, Reanne, Ilana Redstone Akresh, and Bo Lu. 2010. "Latino Immigrants and the US Racial Order: How and Where Do They Fit In?" *American Sociological Review* 75(3): 378–401.

Fries-Britt, Sharon, and Bridget Turner. 2002. "Uneven Stories: Successful Black Collegians at a Black and a White Campus." *Review of Higher Education* 25: 315–30.

Gaddis, S. Michael. 2015. "Discrimination in the Credential Society: An Audit Study of Race and College Selectivity in the Labor Market." *Social Forces* 93(4): 1451–79.

Garbes, Laura. 2021. "When the 'Blank Slate' Is a White One: White Institutional Isomorphism in the Birth of National Public Radio." *Sociology of Race and Ethnicity* 8(1): 79–94.

Glavin, Paul, Scott Schieman, and Sarah Reid. 2011. "Boundary-Spanning Work Demands and Their Consequences for Guilt and Psychological Distress." *Journal of Health and Social Behavior* 52(1): 43–57.

Goldfarb, Nancy D. 2011. "Josiah Royce's Philosophy of Loyalty as Philanthropy." *Nonprofit and Voluntary Sector Quarterly* 40(4): 720–39.

Gomez, Ricardo. 2020. "Success Is Being an Example: Trajectories and Notions of Success among Latinx Faculty, Staff, and Students in Academia." *Journal of Latinos and Education* 19(3): 258–76. doi: 10.1080/15348431.2018.1507909.

Gonzalez, Jorge A., and Angelo S. Denisi. 2009. "Cross-Level Effects of Demography and Diversity Climate on Organizational Attachment and Firm Effectiveness." *Journal of Organizational Behavior: The International Journal of Industrial, Occupational and Organizational Psychology and Behavior* 30(1): 21–40.

Griffin, Kimberly A., Jessica C. Bennett, and Jessica Harris. 2013. "Marginaliz-
ing Merit?: Gender Differences in Black Faculty Discourses on Tenure,
Advancement, and Professional Success." *Review of Higher Education*
36(4): 489–512. doi:10.1353/rhe.2013.0040.

Gurin, Patricia, Eric Dey, Sylvia Hurtado, and Gerald Gurin. 2002. "Diversity
and Higher Education: Theory and Impact on Educational Outcomes."
Harvard Educational Review 72(3): 330–67.

Gurin, Patricia, Biren Ratnesh A. Nagda, and Gretchen E. Lopez. 2004. "The
Benefits of Diversity in Education for Democratic Citizenship." *Journal of
Social Issues* 60(1): 17–34.

Hall, Stuart. 1980. "Race, Articulation, and Societies Structured on Dominance." In *Sociological Theories: Race and Colonialism*, 305–45. Paris:
UNESCO.

Hamilton, Laura T., Kelly Nielsen, and Veronica Lerma. 2022. "'Diversity Is a
Corporate Plan': Racialized Equity Labor among University Employees."
Ethnic and Racial Studies 46(6): 1–23. doi: 10.1080/01419870.2022.2089049.

Haney-Lopez, Ian. 2006. *White by Law: The Legal Construction of Race*. New
York: NYU Press.

Harley, Debra A. 2008. "Maids of Academe: African American Women
Faculty at Predominately White Institutions." *Journal of African American
Studies* 12(1): 19–36.

Harris, Cheryl I. 1993. "Whiteness as Property." *Harvard Law Review* 106(8):
1707–91.

Heffernan, Troy. 2021. "Sexism, Racism, Prejudice, and Bias: A Literature
Review and Synthesis of Research Surrounding Student Evaluations of
Courses and Teaching." *Assessment & Evaluation in Higher Education* 47:
1–11. doi: 10.1080/02602938.2021.1888075.

Herdman, Andrew O., and Amy McMillan-Capehart. 2010 "Establishing a
Diversity Program Is Not Enough: Exploring the Determinants of
Diversity Climate." *Journal of Business and Psychology* 25(1): 39–53.

Herring, Cedric, and Loren Henderson. 2012. "From Affirmative Action to
Diversity: Toward a Critical Diversity Perspective." *Critical Sociology*
38(5): 629–43.

Hirschman, Albert O. 1970. *Exit, Voice, and Loyalty: Responses to Decline in
Firms, Organizations, and States*. Cambridge, MA: Harvard University
Press.

Hitlin, Steven, J. Scott Brown, and Glen H. Elder Jr. 2007. "Measuring Latinos: Racial vs. Ethnic Classification and Self-Understandings." *Social Forces* 86(2): 587–611.

Hodson, Randy. 1996. "Dignity in the Workplace under Participative Management: Alienation and Freedom Revisited." *American Sociological Review* 61(5): 719–38.

Hofhuis, Joep, Karen I. Van der Zee, and Sabine Otten. 2014. "Comparing Antecedents of Voluntary Job Turnover among Majority and Minority Employees." *Equality, Diversity and Inclusion: An International Journal* 33(8): 735–49.

Holder, Aisha M. B., Margo A. Jackson, and Joseph G. Ponterotto. 2015. "Racial Microaggression Experiences and Coping Strategies of Black Women in Corporate Leadership." *Qualitative Psychology* 2(2): 164. doi: 10.1037/qup0000024.

Holland, Megan M., and Karly Sarita Ford. 2021. "Legitimating Prestige through Diversity: How Higher Education Institutions Represent Ethno-Racial Diversity across Levels of Selectivity." *Journal of Higher Education* 92(1): 1–30.

Homan, Astrid C., Daan Van Knippenberg, Gerben A. Van Kleef, and Carsten K. W. De Dreu. 2007. "Bridging Faultlines by Valuing Diversity: Diversity Beliefs, Information Elaboration, and Performance in Diverse Work Groups." *Journal of Applied Psychology* 92(5): 1189.

hooks, bell. 1992. *Black Looks: Race and Representation*. Boston: South End.

Huang, Tiffany J. 2020. "Negotiating the Workplace: Second-Generation Asian American Professionals' Early Experiences." *Journal of Ethnic and Migration Studies* 47(2): 1–20.

Hughey, Matthew W. 2012. "Color Capital, White Debt, and the Paradox of Strong White Racial Identities." *Du Bois Review* 9(1): 169–200.

Hurtado, David A., Erika L. Sabbath, Karen A. Ertel, Orfeu M. Buxton, and Lisa F. Berkman. 2012. "Racial Disparities in Job Strain among American and Immigrant Long-Term Care Workers." *International Nursing Review* 59(2): 237–44. doi: 10.1111/j.1466-7657.2011.00948.x.

Ince, Jelani. 2022. "'Saved' by Interaction, Living by Race: The Diversity Demeanor in an Organizational Space." *Social Psychology Quarterly* 85(3): 259–78. doi: 10.1177/01902725221096373.

Ishimaru, Ann M., and Mollie K. Galloway. 2021. "Hearts and Minds First: Institutional Logics in Pursuit of Educational Equity." *Educational Administration Quarterly* 57(3): 470–502. doi:10.1177/0013161X20947459.

Jackson, Susan E., Aparna Joshi, and Niclas L. Erhardt. 2003. "Recent Research on Team and Organizational Diversity: SWOT Analysis and Implications." *Journal of Management* 29(6): 801–30.

Jaschik, Scott. 2019. "When Colleges Seek Diversity through Photoshop." *Inside Higher Ed*, February 4. Retrieved February 5, 2019. https://www.insidehighered.com/admissions/article/2019/02/04/york-college-pennsylvania-illustrates-issues-when-colleges-change.

Jayakumar, Uma M., and Samuel D. Museus. 2011. "Mapping the Intersection of Campus Cultures and Equitable Outcomes among Racially Diverse Student Populations." In *Creating Campus Cultures: Fostering Success among Racially Diverse Student Populations*, edited by Samuel D. Museus and Uma M. Jayakumar. New York: Routledge.

Joseph, Tiffany D., and Laura E. Hirshfield. 2011. "'Why Don't You Get Somebody New to Do It?' Race and Cultural Taxation in the Academy." *Ethnic and Racial Studies* 34(1): 121–41. doi: 10.1080/01419870.2010.496489.

Joshi, Aparna, Jooyeon Son, and Hyuntak Roh. 2015. "When Can Women Close the Gap? A Meta-analytic Test of Sex Differences in Performance and Rewards." *Academy of Management Journal* 58(5): 1516–45.

Judge, Timothy A., Carl J. Thoresen, Joyce E. Bono, and Gregory K. Patton. 2001. "The Job Satisfaction–Job Performance Relationship: A Qualitative and Quantitative Review." *Psychological Bulletin* 127(3): 376–407.

Kalev, Alexandra, Frank Dobbin, and Erin Kelly. 2006. "Best Practices or Best Guesses? Assessing the Efficacy of Corporate Affirmative Action and Diversity Policies." *American Sociological Review* 71(4): 589–617.

Kalleberg, Arne L. 2011. *Good Jobs, Bad Jobs: The Rise of Polarized and Precarious Employment Systems in the United States, 1970s–2000s*. New York: Russell Sage Foundation.

Kanter, Rosabeth M. 1977. "Some Effects of Proportions on Group Life: Skewed Sex Ratios and Responses to Token Women." *American Journal of Sociology* 82(5): 965–90.

Karasek, Robert, and Tores Theorell. 1990. *Healthy Work: Stress, Productivity, and the Reconstruction of Working Life*. New York: Basic Books.

Kelly, Erin, and Frank Dobbin. 1998. "How Affirmative Action Became Diversity Management: Employer Response to Antidiscrimination Law, 1961 to 1996." *American Behavioral Scientist* 41(7): 960–84.

Kendall, Mikki. 2020. *Hood Feminism: Notes from the Women White Feminists Forgot.* London: Bloomsbury.

Kiang, Lisa, Virginia W. Huynh, Charissa S. L. Cheah, Yijie Wang, and Hirokazu Yoshikawa. 2017. "Moving beyond the Model Minority." *Asian American Journal of Psychology* 8(1): 1.

Koh, Chee Wee, Winny Shen, and Tiffany Lee. 2016. "Black–White Mean Differences in Job Satisfaction: A Meta-analysis." *Journal of Vocational Behavior* 94: 131–43.

Kulik, Carol, and Loriann Roberson. 2008. "Diversity Initiative Effectiveness: What Organizations Can (and Cannot) Expect from Diversity Recruitment, Diversity Training, and Formal Mentoring Programs." In *Diversity at Work*, edited by A. Brief, 265–317. London: Cambridge University Press. http://dx.doi.org/10.1017/CBO9780511753725.010.

Lacy, Karyn R. 2007. *Blue-Chip Black: Race, Class, and Status in the New Black Middle Class.* Berkeley: University of California Press.

Lamont, Michèle. 2000. *The Dignity of Working Men: Morality and the Boundaries of Race, Class, and Immigration.* New York: Russell Sage Foundation.

Lawrence, Andrew. 2024. "'She Endured Cruelty': What Led to a Leader's Death at a Historically Black University?" *The Guardian*, February 28.

Lee, Jennifer, and Frank D. Bean. 2007. "Reinventing the Color Line Immigration and America's New Racial / Ethnic Divide." *Social Forces* 86(2): 561–86.

Lee, Jennifer, and Min Zhou. 2015. *The Asian American Achievement Paradox.* New York: Russell Sage Foundation.

Lee, Jennifer, and Samuel Kye. 2016. "Racialized Assimilation of Asian Americans." *Annual Review of Sociology* 42: 253–73.

Lee, Jennifer, and Dian Sheng. 2023. "The Asian American Assimilation Paradox." *Journal of Ethnic and Migration Studies* 50(2): 1–27. doi: 10.1080/1369183X.2023.2183965.

Lee, Soojung, and Jeongkoo Yoon. 2018. "Does the Authenticity of Corporate Social Responsibility Affect Employee Commitment?" *Social Behavior and Personality: An International Journal* 46(4): 617–32.

Leong, Nancy. 2013. "Racial Capitalism." *Harvard Law Review* 126(8): 2151–226.

Leslie, Lisa M. 2019. "Diversity Initiative Effectiveness: A Typological Theory of Unintended Consequences." *Academy of Management Review* 44(3): 538–63.

Lipson, Daniel N. 2007. "Diversity: The Institutionalization of Affirmative Action as Diversity Management at UC-Berkeley, UT-Austin, and UW-Madison." *Law & Social Inquiry* 32(4): 985–1026.

Lorbiecki, Anna, and Gavin Jack. 2000. "Critical Turns in the Evolution of Diversity Management." *British Journal of Management* 11(1): S17–S31.

Luo, Jiali, and David Jamieson-Drake. 2009. "A Retrospective Assessment of the Educational Benefits of Interaction across Racial Boundaries." *Journal of College Student Development* 50(1): 67–86.

MacLean, Tammy L., and Michael Behnam. 2010. "The Dangers of Decoupling: The Relationship between Compliance Programs, Legitimacy Perceptions, and Institutionalized Misconduct." *Academy of Management Journal* 53(6): 1499–520.

Masci, David. 2018. "5 Facts about Blacks and Religion in America." Pew Research Center, February 7. Retrieved March 25, 2019. https://www.pewresearch.org/fact-tank/2018/02/07/5-facts-about-the-religious-lives-of-african-americans/.

Mayorga-Gallo, Sarah. 2014. *Behind the White Picket Fence: Power and Privilege in a Multiethnic Neighborhood.* Chapel Hill: University of North Carolina Press.

Mayorga-Gallo, Sarah. 2019. "The White-Centering Logic of Diversity Ideology." *American Behavioral Scientist* 63(13): 1789–809.

McMillan Cottom, Tressie. 2015. "'Who Do You Think You Are?': When Marginality Meets Academic Microcelebrity." *Ada: A Journal of Gender, New Media, and Technology* 7(1).

Melaku, Tsedale M. 2019. *You Don't Look Like a Lawyer: Black Women and Systemic Gendered Racism.* Lanham, MD: Rowman & Littlefield.

Melamed, David, Christopher W. Munn, Leanne Barry, Bradley Montgomery, and Oneya F. Okuwobi. 2019. "Status Characteristics, Implicit Bias, and the Production of Racial Inequality." *American Sociological Review* 84(6): 1013–36. doi: 10.1177/0003122419879101.

Melamed, Jodi. 2011. *Represent and Destroy: Rationalizing Violence in the New Racial Capitalism.* Minneapolis: University of Minnesota Press.

Merseth, Julie Lee. 2020. "Race-Ing Solidarity: Asian Americans and Support for Black Lives Matter." In *Asian Pacific American Politics: Celebrating the Scholarly Legacy of Don T. Nakanishi*, edited by Andrew Aoki and Pei-te Lien. Oxfordshire: Routledge.

Meyer, John W., and Brian Rowan. 1977. "Institutionalized Organizations: Formal Structure as Myth and Ceremony." *American Journal of Sociology* 83(2): 340–63.

Minor, James. 2008. "Contemporary HBCUs: Considering Institutional Capacities and State Priorities—A Recent Report." East Lansing: Michigan State University, College of Education, Department of Educational Administration.

Monroe, Kristen R. 1994. "A Fat Lady in a Corset: Altruism and Social Theory." *American Journal of Political Science* 38(4): 861–93.

Moore, Emily L., and J. Herman Blake. 2015. "Inherent Philanthropy in Multicultural Faculty Work at a Research University." In *Faculty Work and the Public Good: Philanthropy, Engagement, and Academic Professionalism*, edited by G. G. Shaker, 97–109. New York: Teachers College Press.

Moore, Wendy Leo. 2008. *Reproducing Racism: White Space, Elite Law Schools, and Racial Inequality*. Lanham, MD: Rowman & Littlefield.

Moore, Wendy Leo, and Joyce M. Bell. 2011. "Maneuvers of Whiteness: 'Diversity' as a Mechanism of Retrenchment in the Affirmative Action Discourse." *Critical Sociology* 37(5): 597–613.

Mor Barak, Michal E., David A. Cherin, and Sherry Berkman. 1988. "Organizational and Personal Dimensions in Diversity Climate: Ethnic and Gender Differences in Employee Perceptions." *Journal of Applied Behavioral Science* 34(1): 82–104.

Mull, Amanda. 2020. "Brands Have Nothing Real to Say about Racism." *The Atlantic*, June 3. Retrieved February 3, 2021. https://www.theatlantic.com/health/archive/2020/06/brands-racism-protests-amazon-nfl-nike/612613/.

Munn, Christopher W. 2017. "The One Friend Rule: Race and Social Capital in an Interracial Network." *Social Problems* 65(4): 473–90.

Munn, Christopher W. 2019. "Finding a Seat at the Table: How Race Shapes Access to Social Capital." *Sociology of Religion* 80(4): 435–55.

Nagel, Thomas. 1970. *The Possibility of Altruism*. Oxford: Clarendon Press.

Niebuhr, Richard, 1956. *The Purpose of the Church and Its Ministry: Reflections on the Aims of Theological Education.* New York: Harper.

Nienhüser, Werner. 2008. "Resource Dependence Theory: How Well Does It Explain Behavior of Organizations?" *Management Revue* 19(1/2): 9–32.

Noah, Trevor (writer); David Paul Meyer (director). 2021. Season 26, episode 80 of *The Daily Show with Trevor Noah.* Executive producers Jill Katz and Jennifer Flanz. MTV Entertainment Studios.

Nomura, Kyoko, Mutsuhiro Nakao, Takeaki Takeuchi, and Eiji Yano. 2009. "Associations of Insomnia with Job Strain, Control, and Support among Male Japanese Workers." *Sleep Medicine* 10(6): 626–29.

Noon, Mike. 2018. "Pointless Diversity Training: Unconscious Bias, New Racism and Agency." *Work, Employment and Society* 32(1): 198–209.

Novac, B.J. (writer); Ken Kwapis (director). 2005. Season 1, episode 2 of *The Office.* Executive producers Ben Silverman, Greg Daniels, Ricky Gervais, Stephen Merchant, Howard Klein, Ken Kwapis, Paul Lieberstein, Jennifer Celotta, B.J. Novak, Mindy Kaling, and Brent Forrester. Reveille Productions and Deedle-Dee Productions.

Noy, Chaim. 2008. "Sampling Knowledge: The Hermeneutics of Snowball Sampling in Qualitative Research." *International Journal of Social Research Methodology* 11(4): 327–44.

Nunley, John M., Adam Pugh, Nicholas Romero, and R. Alan Seals. 2015. "Racial Discrimination in the Labor Market for Recent College Graduates: Evidence from a Field Experiment." *BE Journal of Economic Analysis & Policy* 15(3): 1093–125.

Okorafor, Nnedi. 2019. "Africanfuturism Defined." *Nnedi's Wahala Blog Zone,* October 19. http://nnedi.blogspot.com/2019/10/africanfuturism-defined.html.

Okuwobi, Oneya F. 2019. "'Everything That I've Done Has Always Been Multiethnic': Biographical Work among Leaders of Multiracial Churches." *Sociology of Religion* 80(4): 478–95.

Okuwobi, Oneya F. 2022. "Moving Forward on Race: Trading Cheap Reconciliation for Equity and Unity." In *Red Skies: 10 Essential Conversations Exploring Our Future as the Church,* edited by L. Rowland Smith. Cody, WY: 100 Movements.

Okuwobi, Oneya Fennell. 2024. "Diversity as Philanthropy: Diversity Ideology among Pastors, Professors, and Professionals of Color." *Social Problems* spae008 (February). doi: 10.1093/socpro/spae008.

Okuwobi, Oneya F., Deborwah Faulk, and Vincent Roscigno. 2021. "Diversity Displays and Organizational Messaging: The Case of Historically Black Colleges and Universities." *Sociology of Race and Ethnicity* 7(3): 384-400.

Okuwobi, Oneya F., Bradley Montgomery, and David Melamed. 2023. "Double Consciousness and Racial Status Beliefs." *Social Psychology Quarterly* 86(3): 241-55.

Okuwobi, Oneya Fennell, Christopher W. Munn, and Korie Little Edwards. 2024. "Trading on Diverse Relationships: The Process of Racialized Social Commodification in Multiracial Congregations." *Sociology of Race and Ethnicity* 10(1): 16-30. doi: 10.1177/23326492231213327.

O'Meara, KerryAnn, Liana Sayer, Gudrun Nyunt, and Courtney Lennartz. 2020. "Stressed, Interrupted, and Underestimated: Experiences of Women and URM Faculty during One Workday." *Journal of the Professoriate* 11(1): 105-37.

Omi, Michael, and Howard Winant. 2014. *Racial Formation in the United States*, 3rd ed. New York: Routledge.

Oyakawa, Michelle. 2019. "Racial Reconciliation as a Suppressive Frame in Evangelical Multiracial Churches." *Sociology of Religion* 80(4): 496-517.

Padilla, Amado M. 1994. "Research News and Comment: Ethnic Minority Scholars; Research, and Mentoring: Current and Future Issues." *Educational Researcher* 23(4): 24-27.

Pager, Devah. 2003. "The Mark of a Criminal Record." *American Journal of Sociology* 108(5): 937-75.

Parasuraman, S. 1982. "Predicting Turnover Intentions and Turnover Behavior: A Multivariate Analysis." *Journal of Vocational Behavior* 21(1): 111-21.

Park, Robert 1924. "The Concept of Social Distance as Applied to the Study of Racial Attitudes and Racial Relations." *Journal of Applied Sociology* 8: 339-44.

Patrick, Bethanne. 2021. "An Office Rivalry Turns Strange—and Maybe Dangerous—in 'The Other Black Girl.'" *National Public Radio*, June 4.

Pauly, Megan. 2022. "First Class Enters Maggie Walker School after New Testing Policy Begins." *Virginia Public Media*, August 22. https://vpm.org

/news/articles/35098/first-class-enters-maggie-walker-school-after-new-testing-policy-begins.

Perry, Samuel L. 2012. "Racial Habitus, Moral Conflict, and White Moral Hegemony within Interracial Evangelical Organizations." *Qualitative Sociology* 35(1): 89–108. doi: 10.1007/s11133-011-9215-z.

Petts, Amy L., and Alma Nidia Garza. 2021. "Manipulating Diversity: How Diversity Regimes at US Universities Can Reinforce Whiteness." *Sociology Compass* 15(10): e12925. doi: 10.1111/soc4.12925.

Pfeffer, Jeffrey, and G. R. Salancik. 1978. *The External Control of Organizations: A Resource Dependence Perspective*. New York: Harper & Row.

Pippert, Timothy D., Laura J. Essenburg, and Edward J. Matchett. 2013. "We've Got Minorities, Yes We Do: Visual Representations of Racial and Ethnic Diversity in College Recruitment Materials." *Journal of Marketing for Higher Education* 23(2): 258–82.

Pitt, Richard N. 2012. *Divine Callings: Understanding the Call to Ministry in Black Pentecostalism*. New York: NYU Press.

Portocarrero, Sandra. 2023. "Racialized Expertise: The Consequences of Perceiving the Race of Workers as a Type of Expertise." *Academy of Management Proceedings* 2023(1): 16280. doi: 10.5465/AMPROC.2023.1bp.

Press, Eyal. 2021. *Dirty Work: Essential Jobs and the Hidden Toll of Inequality in America*. New York: Farrar, Straus and Giroux.

Quillian, Lincoln, Devah Pager, Ole Hexel, and Arnfinn H. Midtbøen. 2017. "Meta-Analysis of Field Experiments Shows No Change in Racial Discrimination in Hiring over Time." *Proceedings of the National Academy of Sciences* 114(41): 10870–75.

Quiroz-Gutierrez, Marco. 2021. "The Top 20 Fortune 500 Companies on Diversity and Inclusion." June 2. Retrieved October 21, 2021. https://fortune.com/2021/06/02/fortune-500-companies-diversity-inclusion-numbers-refinitiv-measure-up/.

Ray, Victor. 2019. "A Theory of Racialized Organizations." *American Sociological Review* 84(1): 26–53.

Ray, Victor. 2019. "Why So Many Organizations Stay White." *Harvard Business Review*, November 19. https://hbr.org/2019/11/why-so-many-organizations-stay-white.

Ray, Victor, Antonia Randolph, Megan Underhill, and David Luke. 2017. "Critical Race Theory, Afro-Pessimism, and Racial Progress Narratives." *Sociology of Race and Ethnicity* 3(2): 147–58.

Reskin, Barbara. 2012. "The Race Discrimination System." *Annual Review of Sociology* 38(1): 17–35.

Richeson, Jennifer A., Sophie Trawalter, and J. Nicole Shelton. 2005. "African Americans' Implicit Racial Attitudes and the Depletion of Executive Function after Interracial Interactions." *Social Cognition* 23(4): 336–52.

Ridgeway, Cecilia L., and Henry A. Walker. 1995. "Status Structures." In *Sociological Perspectives on Social Psychology*, edited by K.S. Cook, G.A. Fine, and J.S. House, 281–310. Boston: Allyn and Bacon.

Roberson, Quinetta M., and Hyeon Jeong Park. 2007. "Examining the Link between Diversity and Firm Performance: The Effects of Diversity Reputation and Leader Racial Diversity." *Group & Organization Management* 32(5): 548–68.

Robinson, Cedric J. 2000. *Black Marxism: The Making of the Black Radical Tradition*. Chapel Hill: University of North Carolina Press.

Robinson, Tilly, and Neil Shah. 2024. "Harvard Faculty of Arts and Sciences Will No Longer Require Diversity Statements." *Harvard Crimson*, June 4. Retrieved June 5, 2024. https://www.thecrimson.com/article/2024/6/4/dei-faculty-hiring-stopped/.

Rock, Chris, interviewee. 2020. Season 26, episode 14 of *The Daily Show with Trevor Noah*. MTV Entertainment Studios.

Roscigno, Vincent, and Jill E. Yavorsky. 2014. "Discrimination, Diversity and Work." In *Routledge International Handbook of Diversity Studies*, edited by Steven Vertovec. New York: Routledge.

Schoon, Eric W. 2022. "Operationalizing Legitimacy." *American Sociological Review* 87(3): 478–503. doi: 10.1177/00031224221081379.

Segura, Denise A. 2003. "Navigating between Two Worlds: The Labyrinth of Chicana Intellectual Production in the Academy." *Journal of Black Studies* 34(1): 28–51.

Severson, Annabelle Moore, Morgan. 2024. "Women, Black Staffers Affected Most by UT Austin DEI Cuts." *Houston Chronicle*. Retrieved June 4, 2024. https://www.houstonchronicle.com/politics/texas/article/ut-dei-layoffs-19410906.php.

Shaban, Hamza. 2020. "Wells Fargo CEO Apologizes after Disparaging Black Talent Pool." *Washington Post*, September 23. Retrieved March 26, 2022. https://www.washingtonpost.com/business/2020/09/23/wells-fargo-ceo-black-employees/.

Shim, J. 2020. "Token Fatigue: Tolls of Marginalization in White Male Spaces." *Ethnic and Racial Studies* 44(7): 1115–34.

Singh, Barjinder, and T. T. Selvarajan. 2013. "Is It Spillover or Compensation? Effects of Community and Organizational Diversity Climates on Race Differentiated Employee Intent to Stay." *Journal of Business Ethics* 115(2): 259–69.

Smith, Belinda J. 2020. "12 Years a Diversity Hire." Medium. Retrieved June 5, 2024. https://medium.com/@belindasmiths/12-years-a-diversity-hire-44b9804a331b.

Smith, Candis Watts, and Sarah Mayorga-Gallo. 2017. "The New Principle-Policy Gap: How Diversity Ideology Subverts Diversity Initiatives." *Sociological Perspectives* 60(5): 889–911.

Smith, Paige. 2022. "Wells Fargo to Pay $7.8 Million to Settle Hiring Bias Claims." *Bloomberg*. Retrieved December 26, 2022. https://news.bloomberglaw.com/daily-labor-report/wells-fargo-to-pay-7-8-million-to-settle-hiring-bias-claims.

Sobering, Katherine. 2019. "The Relational Production of Workplace Equality: The Case of Worker-Recuperated Businesses in Argentina." *Qualitative Sociology* 42(4): 543–65. doi: 10.1007/s11133-019-09434-y.

Spector, Paul E. 1986. "Perceived Control by Employees: A Meta-analysis of Studies Concerning Autonomy and Participation at Work." *Human Relations* 39(11): 1005–16.

Stainback, Kevin, and Donald Tomaskovic-Devey. 2012. *Documenting Desegregation: Racial and Gender Segregation in Private Sector Employment since the Civil Rights Act*. New York: Russell Sage Foundation.

Stichman, Amy J., Kimberly D. Hassell, and Carol A. Archbold. 2010. "Strength in Numbers? A Test of Kanter's Theory of Tokenism." *Journal of Criminal Justice* 38(4): 633–39.

Stinchcombe, Arthur L. 1965. "Organization-Creating Organizations." *Trans-Actions* 2(1): 34–35.

Sull, Donald, Charles Sull, and Ben Zweig. 2022. "Toxic Culture Is Driving the Great Resignation." *MIT Sloan Management Review*, January 11.

Thomas, James M. 2019. "The Economization of Diversity." *Sociology of Race and Ethnicity* 5(4): 471–85.

Thomas, James M. 2020. *Diversity Regimes: Why Talk Is Not Enough to Fix Racial Inequality at Universities.* New Brunswick, NJ: Rutgers University Press.

Thomson, Robert A., Esmeralda Sánchez Salazar, and Elaine Howard Ecklund. 2021. "The Very Ivory Tower: Pathways Reproducing Racial-Ethnic Stratification in US Academic Science." *Ethnic and Racial Studies* 44(7): 1250–70. doi: 10.1080/01419870.2020.1786144.

Thumma, Scott, and Dave Travis. 2007. *Beyond Megachurch Myths: What We Can Learn from America's Largest Churches.* San Francisco: John Wiley & Sons.

Tomaskovic-Devey, Donald, and Dustin Avent-Holt. 2019. *Relational Inequalities: An Organizational Approach.* New York: Oxford University Press.

Trawalter, Sophie, Sara Driskell, and Martin N. Davidson. 2016. "What Is Good Isn't Always Fair: On the Unintended Effects of Framing Diversity as Good." *Analyses of Social Issues and Public Policy* 16(1): 69–99. doi: 10.1111/asap.12103.

Tulshyan, Ruchika. 2021. "Return to Office? Some Women of Color Aren't Ready." *New York Times*, June 23.

Umaña-Taylor, Adriana J., and Nana Shin. 2007. "An Examination of Ethnic Identity and Self-Esteem with Diverse Populations: Exploring Variation by Ethnicity and Geography." *Cultural Diversity and Ethnic Minority Psychology* 13: 178–86. doi: 10.1037/1099-9809.13.2.178.

United States Supreme Court. 1978. *Regents of the University of California v. Bakke.* University Publications of America.

Uwan, Ekemini. 2019. "The Blood of Jesus Is the Bridge; Not My Back." Retrieved August 12, 2021. https://www.sistamatictheology.com/blog1/2019/4/7/the-blood-of-jesus-is-the-bridge-not-my-back.

Valente, Rubia R., and Brian J. L. Berry. 2017. "Acculturation of Immigrant Latinos into the U.S. Workplace: Evidence from the Working Hours-Life Satisfaction Relationship." *Applied Research in Quality of Life* 12(2): 451–79. doi: 10.1007/s11482-016-9471-x.

Vallejo, Jody. 2015. "Levelling the Playing Field: Patterns of Ethnic Philanthropy among Los Angeles' Middle- and Upper-Class Latino Entrepreneurs." *Ethnic and Racial Studies* 38(1): 125–40. doi: 10.1080/01419870.2013.848288.

Van Knippenberg, Daan, and Michaela C. Schippers. 2007. "Work Group Diversity." *Annual Review of Psychology* 58(1): 515–41.

Warikoo, Natasha K. 2016. *The Diversity Bargain: and Other Dilemmas of Race, Admissions, and Meritocracy at Elite Universities*. Chicago: University of Chicago Press.

Wilson, William Julius. 1987. *The Truly Disadvantaged: The Inner City, The Underclass, and Public Policy*. Chicago: University of Chicago Press.

Wingfield, Adia Harvey. 2009. "Racializing the Glass Escalator: Reconsidering Men's Experiences with Women's Work." *Gender & Society* 23(1): 5–26. doi: 10.1177/0891243208323054.

Wingfield, Adia Harvey. 2013. *No More Invisible Man: Race and Gender in Men's Work*. Philadelphia: Temple University Press.

Wingfield, Adia Harvey. 2019. *Flatlining: Race, Work, and Health Care in the New Economy*. Oakland: University of California Press.

Wingfield, Adia Harvey, and Renée Skeete Alston. 2014. "Maintaining Hierarchies in Predominantly White Organizations: A Theory of Racial Tasks." *American Behavioral Scientist* 58(2): 274–87. doi: 10.1177/0002764213503329.

Wolfe, John T. 2015. "The Skin I Am In: A Perspective on Diversity in Historically Black Colleges and Universities." In *Exploring Issues of Diversity within HBCUs*, edited by T. N. Ingram, D. Greenfield, J. D. Carter, and A. A. Hilton, 7–36. Charlotte, NC: Information Age.

Wooten, Melissa E. 2015. *In the Face of Inequality: How Black Colleges Adapt*. Reprint ed. Albany: State University of New York Press.

Wooten, Melissa E., and Lucius Couloute. 2017. "The Production of Racial Inequality within and among Organizations." *Sociology Compass* 11(1): e12446. doi: 10.1111/soc4.12446.

Wright, Eric O. 2011. "Real Utopias." *Contexts* 10(2): 36–42.

Wuthnow, Robert J. 2011. "Taking Talk Seriously: Religious Discourse as Social Practice." *Journal for the Scientific Study of Religion* 50(1): 1–21. doi: 10.1111/j.1468-5906.2010.01549.x.

Yancey, George, and Ye Jung Kim. 2008. "Racial Diversity, Gender Equality, and SES Diversity in Christian Congregations: Exploring the Connections of Racism, Sexism, and Classism in Multiracial and Nonmultiracial Churches." *Journal for the Scientific Study of Religion* 47(1): 103–11.

Yoder, Janice D. 1991. "Rethinking Tokenism: Looking beyond Numbers." *Gender and Society* 5(1): 178–92.

Zimmer, Lynn 1988. "Tokenism and Women in the Workplace: The Limits of Gender-Neutral Theory." *Social Problems* 35(1): 64–77.

Index

job strain, 65–68; commodification, 67, 85, 185; diversity ideology, 82; emotional and physical symptoms, 185; and family, 79; and job involvement, 85–87; social support, 83, 88, 92; work / family conflict. *See also* stress

Johnson, Lyndon B., 10

Johnson, Pastor James, 78–79, 201

Johnson, Professor Sam, 117–119, 202

Kalev, Alexandra, 165, 218n15

Kalleburg, Arne, 87

Kanter, Rosabeth Moss, 42–43

Lacaba, Tea, 107–108, 110, 112, 188, 190, 203

Latinas/os: academic labor demands, 56, 66; Afro Latinos, 102; diversity offices, 179; and other employees of color, 90, 97–98, 104; pastor, 58; radio station programming, 155

Latino Studies, 154

legitimacy: commodification, 13, 88, 139, 182, 185, 191; differential, 212n7; diversity as resource, 111, 138; external, 34, 39–40; internal, 18, 33–34, 48, 55, 82, 166; threats to personal, 31–32, 37, 55–56, 63–64, 72, 92; pressures, 160; racial equity, 182, 194–195; racial incidents, 97, 170; subjugated identity, 105; "window dressing," 177. *See also* increased job demands

Leong, Nancy, 17, 81

Lerma, Veronica, 112, 187

lumping together, 22

"maids of academe," 56

Mar, Alma, 131–133, 137, 140

marginalization, 44, 53–54, 103–104

Marshall, Ayodele, 29, 202; commodification, 30–31, 119; issues of legitimacy, 32, 34; serving majority Black constituencies, 41, 119–121; subjugated identity, 35

Master of Divinity, 7

mentorship: Black faculty and other people of color, 3, 126, 133; disproportionate work for Black faculty, 96, 98, 101, 113–114; lack of support for employees of color, 28, 173; organizational support for, 181; outside of one's field, 171–172

Merseth, Julie Lee, 216n14

Mexican American, 102

microaggressions, 100

Mid-Atlantic, 149

middle class, 23, 129; affirmative action, 23; collective uplift, 124; costs of diversity, 6, 198; whiteness, 22, 146

Midwest, 45, 93, 129; church, 161, 193; faculty, 33, 56, 86, 98, 173, 176; liberal arts college, 102, 126; research university, 121, 123; small university, 127, 131

ministry: associate pastors, 21; career, 7, 142; children's, 162; critique of diverse churches, 196; status and fundraising, 144; student, 48; vocational, 188, 194, 214n25; women's pastor, 58. *See also* "calling"

model minority myth, 92, 94, 215n7

Montague, Orinthia T., 67

Founded in 1893,
UNIVERSITY OF CALIFORNIA PRESS
publishes bold, progressive books and journals
on topics in the arts, humanities, social sciences,
and natural sciences—with a focus on social
justice issues—that inspire thought and action
among readers worldwide.

The UC PRESS FOUNDATION
raises funds to uphold the press's vital role
as an independent, nonprofit publisher, and
receives philanthropic support from a wide
range of individuals and institutions—and from
committed readers like you. To learn more, visit
ucpress.edu/supportus.

www.ingramcontent.com/pod-product-compliance
Lightning Source LLC
Chambersburg PA
CBHW020846270326
41928CB00006B/572